Chicken GAMES & PUZZLES

100 Word Games, Picture Puzzles, Fun Mazes, Silly Jokes, Codes, and Activities for Kids

Illustrated by
Patrick Merrell

Storey Publishing

The mission of Storey Publishing is to serve our customers by publishing practical information that encourages personal independence in harmony with the environment.

Edited by Lisa H. Hiley
Cover and book design by Patrick Merrell
Front cover photography by © Anatoli Tsekhmister/iStockphoto.com (chick), © Eric Isselée/iStockphoto.com (hen), and © Nick Schlax/iStockphoto.com (pencil)

Storey Publishing
210 MASS MoCA Way
North Adams, MA 01247
www.storey.com

Printed in the United States by Versa Press
10 9 8 7 6 5 4

What small type.

Dedicated to
Nancy, Doug,
and
COOP
(Chicken Owners Outside ^ Philadelphia)
and in

Contents

The puzzles increase in difficulty as you go.

Welcome!

Hi, I'm Rudy!
And I'm Buttercup!
We'll be keeping you company throughout this book.
We'll even offer some helpful tips now and then.
The first tip is to read the instructions on the next page.

The puzzles get a little tougher as you go through the sections. Start at the beginning of the book and work your way up, or hunt and peck around. It's up to you!

There's a chicken Dictionary Quiz at the end that will test how many chicken words you know. Every word in the dictionary appears in one of the puzzles in this book.

A few suggestions:

- Use a pencil in case you need to erase.
- Do the puzzles and games alone, or with others – whatever is more fun for you.
- It's okay to take a peek at the answers if you're stuck. We won't tell!
- Most important – have fun!

Hey, Buttercup, you didn't even look at this page!

FUN
Boring Stuff
Hey, wait for me!

DAWN

Wake Up!
Time to Start Solving

DIFFICULTY RATING:

1 Egg

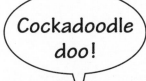

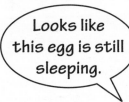

Cockadoodle doo!

Looks like this egg is still sleeping.

Hee hee.

Breakfast!

Help Rudy and Buttercup find the fresh pile of scraps so they can pick through it. If your path takes you to some other item, you'll have to back up.

End

Start

Checking In

Circle all the words with a ✔ in front of them.
Then read down to find a riddle and answer.

✤WHY ★WHO ✦WHERE ✔WHICH ☞WHOSE ✲WHAT

✦RIM ☞EDGE ✤TEAM ★END ✲LINE ✔SIDE

✔OF ★OFF ☞ON ✦OR ✲IF ✤OUT

★TWO ✔A ☞AN ✦AS ✲AT ✤ONE

✲DUCK ✦TURKEY ✤RABBIT ☞HOG ✔CHICKEN ★GOAT

✲OWNS ☞HAD ✔HAS ✤WANTS ★KEEPS ✦NEEDS

☞LEAST ✲FEWER ✦BEST ✤WORST ✔MORE ✠LESS

✤COMBS? ☞TAILS? ✦FEET? ✲FACES? ★LEGS? ✔FEATHERS?

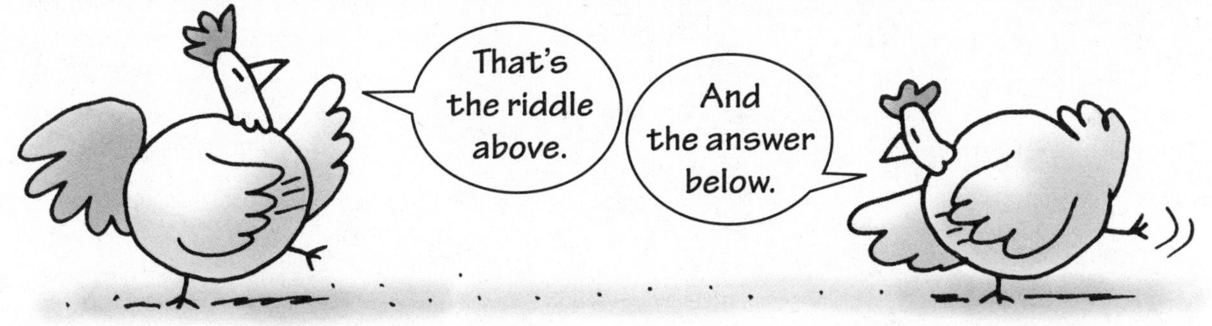

That's the riddle above.
And the answer below.

✦THIS ✔THE ★THAN ☞THEY ✲THESE ✤THEM

✲INSIDE ☞EASTSIDE ✔OUTSIDE ★OFFSIDE ✤UPSIDE

Off-Course

Change each letter below to the one that comes just BEFORE it in the alphabet. Write each new letter on the line above the original letter. When you're done, you'll find a riddle and its answer.

Here is a copy of the alphabet to help you:

A B C D E F G H I J K L M N O P Q R S T U V W X Y Z

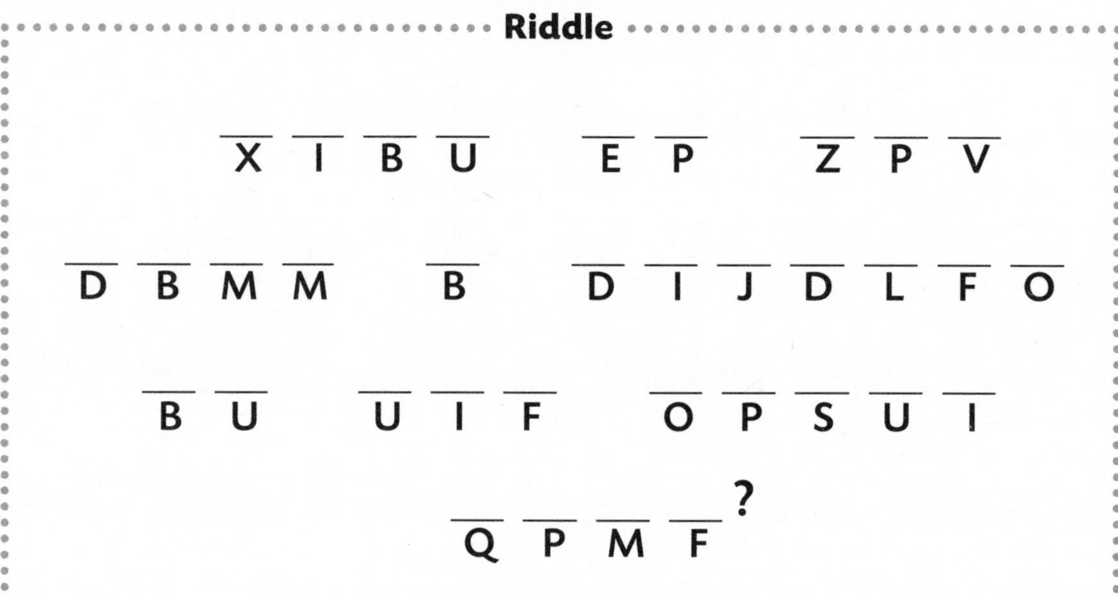

Riddle
X I B U E P Z P V
D B M M B D I J D L F O
B U U I F O P S U I
Q P M F ?

Answer
M P T U
Mush!
Mush? I thought this was snow!

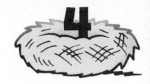

Order! Order!

Can you put these six pictures in order so they make sense?
Write the numbers from 1 to 6 in the circles.

Wake-Up Call

Each word on the left contains one letter that's not in the word to its right. Write the extra letter on the blank. Then read down the gray column to answer this riddle:

What do you call a rooster who wakes you at the same time every morning?

WAITER	___	WRITE
LISTEN	___	TILES
CASHEW	___	CHEWS
STAPLE	___	PASTE
TURBAN	___	BRUNT
REGRET	___	GREET
SIMMER	___	MISER
MUSCLE	___	MULES
HALVES	___	SHAVE
UMPIRE	___	PRIME
CASTLE	___	LEAST
TAKING	___	GIANT

Hmm ...
a letter that's
in WAITER but not
in WRITE?

Egg Collecting

Players take turns. On each turn, draw a short line to connect two dots. When you complete a triangle to surround an egg, mark your initials on that egg. The person who collects (initials) the most eggs wins.

Yum or Yuck!

Five of these things are good for hens to eat. If you've never been around a farm, one or two of the correct answers might surprise you. Circle the five things you think a hen would say YUM! to.

Grain

Brick

Alfalfa

Crushed oyster shell

Dirt

Look at the words on the first line to find the one letter that's used only once. That letter is "M," which has been written in the first space below. Do the same thing with the other lines. Then read across to find a good source of protein for chickens.

1.	SEEM	SOLE	LESS	LOSS
2.	HILL	THIN	LINE	HINT
3.	WILD	DOWN	LOAN	WIND
4.	SALT	TEST	MEAT	TEEM
5.	RACE	CARE	CROW	CORE
6.	LIPS	POLE	PEST	TILL
7.	WOLF	ROLL	FLOW	FOWL
8.	DIET	LIME	TIDE	DELL
9.	MOPE	MANE	SNAP	POEM

Answer: M E A L W O R M S
1 2 3 4 5 6 7 8 9

What's the Difference?

There are 10 differences between the drawing on the left page and the one on this page. Can you find them all?

Find My Dad!

Which rooster is this chick's father? Read through the list and cross off any rooster that doesn't match. Do it correctly and you'll be left with just one rooster – the chick's father!

My dad ...

... has a comb on top of his head

... doesn't have speckled feathers

... has a dark-colored tail

... can't raise his wings above his head

... isn't skinny

... never runs anywhere

... isn't any bigger than his pals

comb

1 2 3 4 5 6 7 8

Mirror Mirror

Take a solving break! Hold this page up to a mirror to find three riddles and their answers.

WHY DID THE CHICKEN CROSS THE PLAYGROUND?

TO GET TO THE OTHER SLIDE.

WHY DID THE CHICKEN CROSS THE INTERNET?

TO GET TO THE OTHER SITE.

WHY DID THE HORSE CROSS THE ROAD?

THE CHICKEN NEEDED A DAY OFF.

Hey, Rudy, come on over to this side of the road.

Move It

Move the letters listed below to the correct spaces. For example, C gets moved to spaces 8, 11, 32, and 36. When all the letters have been moved you'll find a riddle and answer.

C = 8, 11, 32, 36
D = 6, 26
E = 3, 5, 13, 21, 22, 24, 31
G = 16
H = 2, 9
I = 10, 35
K = 12, 23, 33
N = 14, 19, 25, 29, 34
O = 7, 17, 18, 28
P = 30
R = 4
S = 15, 27, 37
W = 1, 20

Move the letters into these spaces:

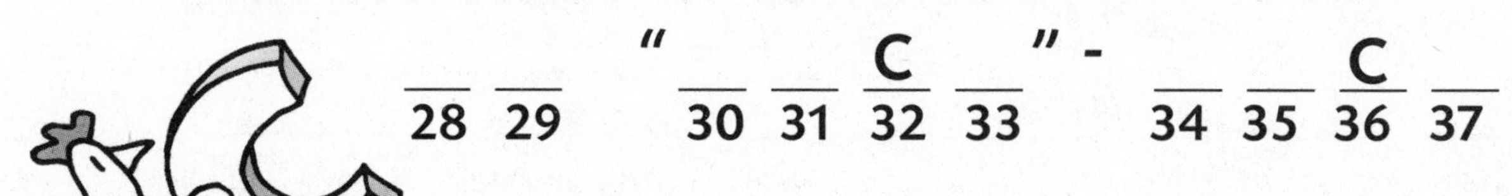

Picture This

Write the name of each picture on the blanks above it. Then transfer only the numbered letters to the blanks at the bottom of the page. Read across to find the name of a chicken breed.

A. ___ ___ ___ ___ ___
(numbered blanks: 2nd = 1, 3rd = 8, 4th = 7)

B. ___ ___ ___ ___ ___
(numbered blanks: 1st = 6)

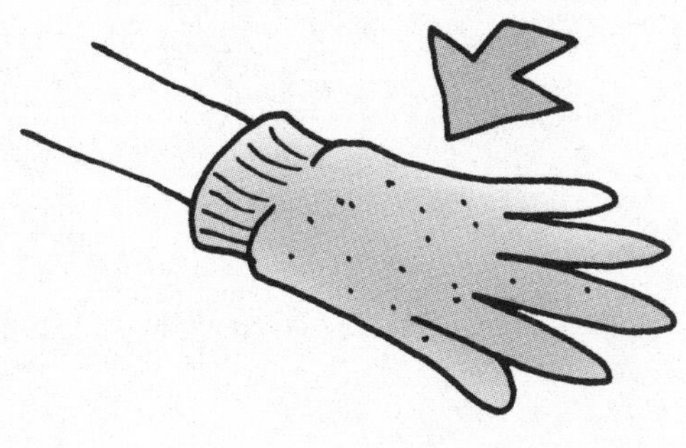

C. ___ ___ ___ ___ ___
(numbered blanks: 2nd = 3, 3rd = 2, 5th = 9)

D. ___ ___ ___ ___ ___ ___
(numbered blanks: 2nd = 4, 3rd = 5)

Answer: ___ ___ ___ ___ ___ ___ ___ ___ ___
1 2 3 4 5 6 7 8 9

This breed of chicken is friendly, tame, and quite popular.

Barnyard Dash

Rudy and Buttercup have laid out some fence posts to make a twisty trail across the barnyard. Can you find the one way through it?

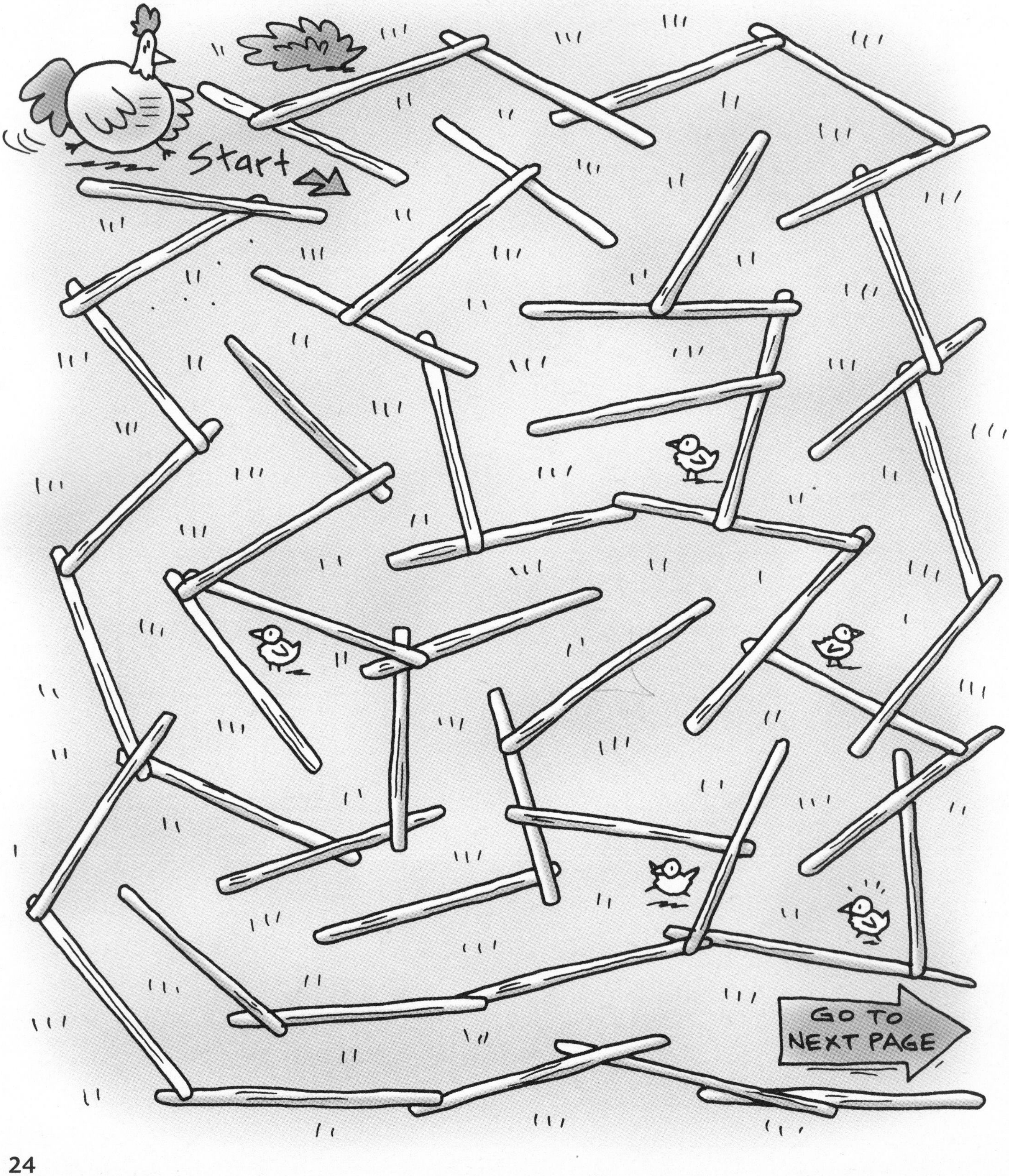

Start

GO TO NEXT PAGE

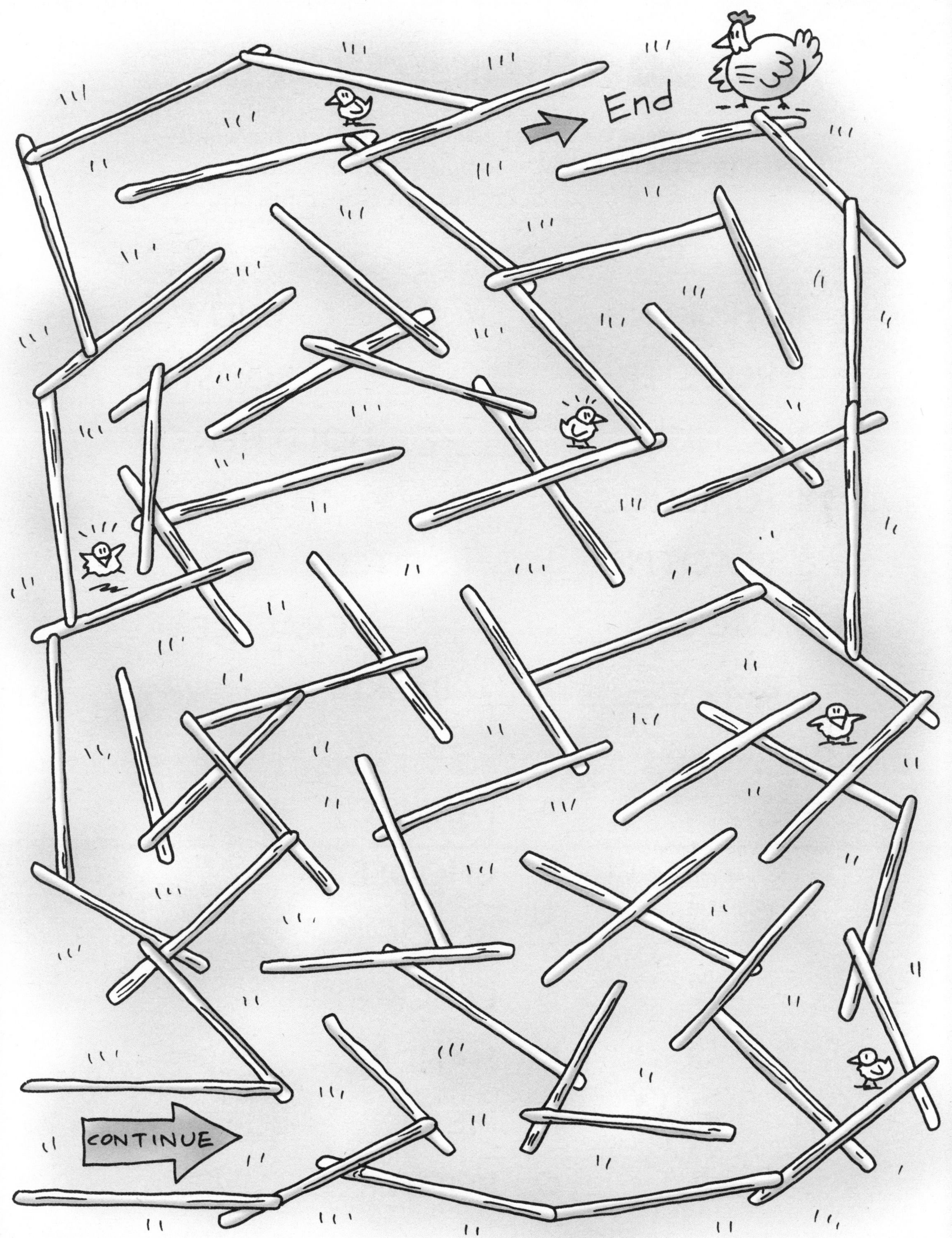
End
CONTINUE

14

Beak Breakers

Each tongue twister is missing a word. Fill in the words from the list below to complete the tongue twisters, then see if you can say each one three times fast.

1. CHICKENS _ _ _ _ _ _ CHOW
2. ROOSTER _ _ _ _ _ _ BOOSTER
3. WHOSE _ _ _ _ _ HOLD HENS
4. FUMBLING _ _ _ _ _ _ _
5. PEACH PIT _ _ _ PITCH
6. CACKLE, _ _ _ _ _, CRACKLE
7. BIG _ _ _ _ _ BASKET

Careful — saying these tongue twisters might break your beak.

A. FARMBOY
B. CHOOSE
C. BLACK
D. CLUCK
E. HANDS
F. PIE
G. ROOTER

Or at least bend it a little!

Starting Line

Fill in each blank to make a word that finishes the sentence. Then read down the column to describe someone who's very likable.

The fourth month of the year is... A PRIL

The color of broccoli is... G REEN

A large body of water is called an... O CEAN

The opposite of closed is... O PEN

Another term for 12 is one... D OZEN

The number after ten is... E LEVEN

A door in a fence is called a... G ATE

A car can be parked in a... G ARAGE

Choices

Are you looking for the perfect chicken pet for you and your family? Here are just a few of the breeds available. Put each one into the grid using the starting letter as your guide. Happy choosing!

ANCONA
BRAHMA
BUCKEYE
DELAWARE
DUTCH
HAMBURG
REDCAP
SILKIE

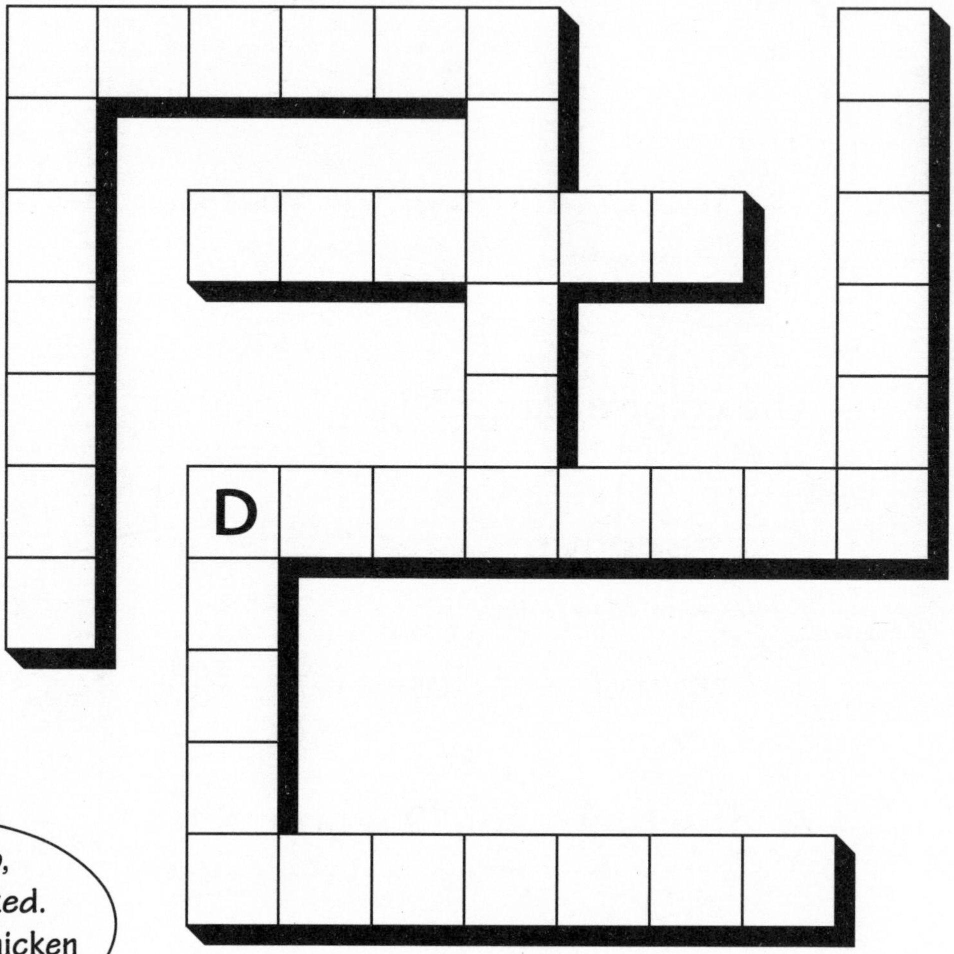

D

Buttercup, I've never asked. What kind of chicken are you?

A cartoon chicken.

House Mates

Only one of these hen houses has an exact copy below.
Look carefully and see if you can figure out which one it is.

Name that Chick

Many chicken owners love to give their pets unusual names. Here are 11 of them. Look across and down, both forward and backward, in the grid for each word and circle it when you find it. FLUFF is circled and crossed off the word list to start you off.

Look for these words:

- COOPS
- EGGATHA
- EGGBERT
- FEATHER
- FLUFF
- HENNY
- LULU
- PEPPER
- ROSY
- RUSTY
- SHELLY

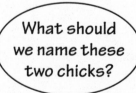

What should we name these two chicks?

Cheep.
cheep cheep.

How about Cheep and Cheeper.

Triple Treat

The words to three silly riddles are mixed together. To read these riddles and their answers, look for different letter styles. First, find all the words written in the "**HOW**" style and write them in order on the first two lines. Do the same thing two more times and then you can crack up!

HOW	DID	**What**	**do**	*WHICH*	**you**
FAIRY	**get**	THE	EGG	*TALES*	CROSS
ARE	**if**	**you**	THE	**cross**	**a**
THE	ROAD?	**hen**	*BEST?*	IT	*THE*
with	*ONES*	SCRAMBLED	*WITH*	*HAPPY*	
a	**dog?**	*EGGINGS.*	**Pooched**	ACROSS.	**eggs.**

1. ____

____

2. ____

____

3. ____

____

GAME

Cross the Road

A game for 1 to 6 players using one die. Can you get across the road and all the way to the finish? Follow the rules on the next page and find out!

1 RANDOLPH	SCRATCH THE GROUND		CACKLE LIKE A HEN	CROW LIKE A ROOSTER
2 MARTHA	CROW LIKE A ROOSTER		PECK AT THIS SPACE	SCRATCH THE GROUND
3 HERB	PECK AT THIS SPACE	FLAP YOUR WINGS		CACKLE LIKE A HEN
4 LUWANDA		CACKLE LIKE A HEN	SCRATCH THE GROUND	
5 MALCOLM	FLAP YOUR WINGS		CROW LIKE A ROOSTER	SCRATCH THE GROUND
6 GIZZY		CROW LIKE A ROOSTER		FLAP YOUR WINGS

THE

ROAD

1. Pick a chicken and write your initials in the numbered starting square. If you're playing alone, pick 3 chickens. The other 3 will be ours.
2. Roll the die. The player whose number comes up moves forward one square (write your initials anywhere in the next square).
3. If you come to a square with writing in it, do what it says.
4. First to the finish wins! *Note*: THE ROAD counts as one square.

		PECK AT THIS SPACE		FLAP YOUR WINGS	**Y**
		CACKLE LIKE A HEN	FLAP YOUR WINGS		**O**
	SCRATCH THE GROUND		CROW LIKE A ROOSTER		**U**
	CROW LIKE A ROOSTER	FLAP YOUR WINGS		PECK AT THIS SPACE	**W**
	PECK AT THIS SPACE		CACKLE LIKE A HEN		**I**
	CACKLE LIKE A HEN	PECK AT THIS SPACE		SCRATCH THE GROUND	**N**

Threesies

Cross off every letter that appears in the grid THREE times. Then put the LEFTOVER letters in the blank spaces below. Go from left to right and top to bottom to find the country that has the most chickens in the world.

B	G	V	S	J	C	D
E	T	Y	Z	R	T	R
Z	R	X	H	Z	D	V
E	L	T	W	W	W	L
I	V	M	D	S	Q	O
J	Y	G	M	N	S	E
O	Q	X	Y	M	O	G
B	X	A	L	J	Q	B

Answer:

__ __ __ __ __

DAY 2

Stretch Your Legs — and Your Brain

DIFFICULTY RATING:

2 Eggs

P-P-Puzzle

There are at least 15 common words in this picture that start with the letter P. Can you find 10 or more?

The Mayflower Chicken

Write a letter in the blank space to complete each seven-letter word. Then read down the gray column to find a popular breed of chicken whose name is the same as a famous historical spot.

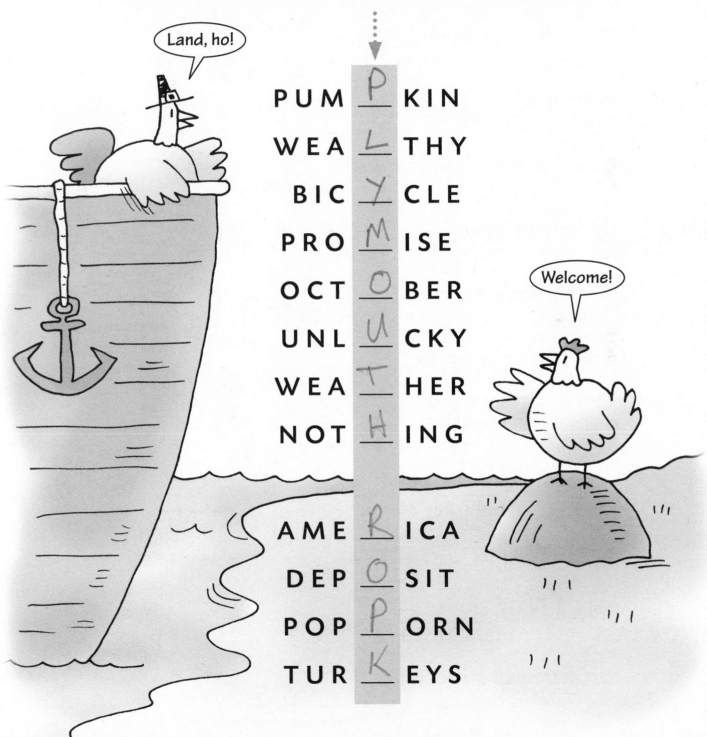

Land, ho!

PUM _P_ KIN

WEA _L_ THY

BIC _Y_ CLE

PRO _M_ ISE

OCT _O_ BER

UNL _U_ CKY

WEA _T_ HER

NOT _H_ ING

Welcome!

AME _R_ ICA

DEP _O_ SIT

POP _P_ ORN

TUR _K_ EYS

Riddle Fun

Write the answer to each clue in the numbered blanks. Then move each letter to the same-numbered space in the box on the next page. Work back and forth between the clues and the box to find a riddle and its answer.

This one is as easy as ...

The month after April: ___ ___ ___
49 3 7

Very large: ___ ___ ___
30 17 54

Dessert with filling and a crust: ___ ___ ___
16 13 11

Opposite of love: ___ ___ ___ ___
41 19 12 45

Came in first in a contest: ___ ___ ___
1 42 29

This card can also be the lowest one in the deck.

A short sleep for babies: ___ ___ ___
35 39 33

Highest card in a deck: ___ ___ ___
50 26 53

Those people: ___ ___ ___ ___
4 24 38 32

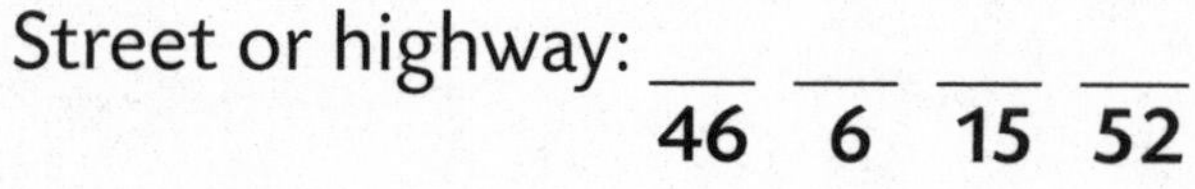

Street or highway: ___ ___ ___ ___
46 6 15 52

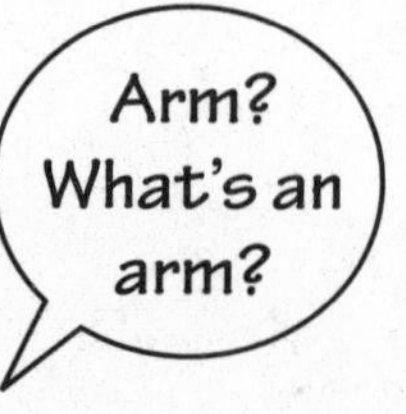

"That hurts!": ___ ___ ___ ___
37 31 23 47

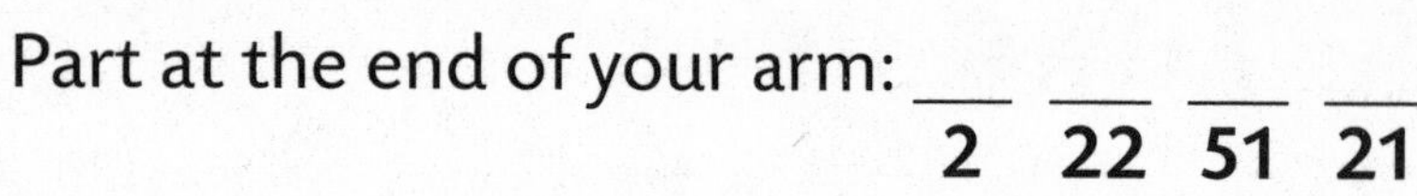

Part at the end of your arm: ___ ___ ___ ___
2 22 51 21

___mare (bad dream): ___ ___ ___ ___ ___
20 25 10 44 36

Not feeling well: ___ ___ ___ ___
56 34 40 27

Hot ____ sundae (chocolate treat): ___ ___ ___ ___ ___
14 9 5 55 28

Farm animal with horns: ___ ___ ___ ___
18 8 48 43

Riddle:

1 2 3 4   5 6   7 8 9

10 11 12   13 14   15

16 17 18   19 20 21   22

23 24 25 26 27 28 29   30 31 32 33

34 35 36 37   38 39 40 41   42 43 44 45 46?

Riddle answer:

47 48 49   50 51 52   53 54 55 56.

Just Joking

Change each letter below to the one that comes just BEFORE it in the alphabet. Write each new letter on the line above the original letter. When you're done, you'll find two riddles and answers.

Here is a copy of the alphabet to help you:

A B C D E F G H I J K L M N O P Q R S T U V W X Y Z

Riddle 1:

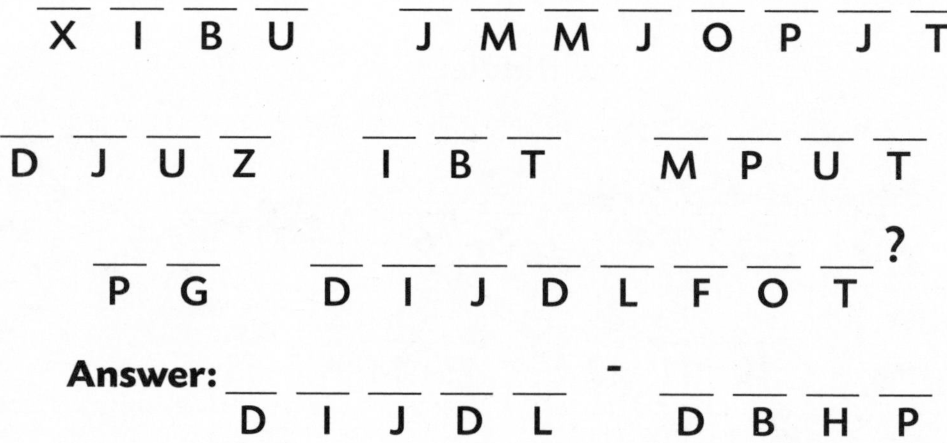

X I B U J M M J O P J T
D J U Z I B T M P U T
P G D I J D L F O T ?
Answer: D I J D L - D B H P

Riddle 2:

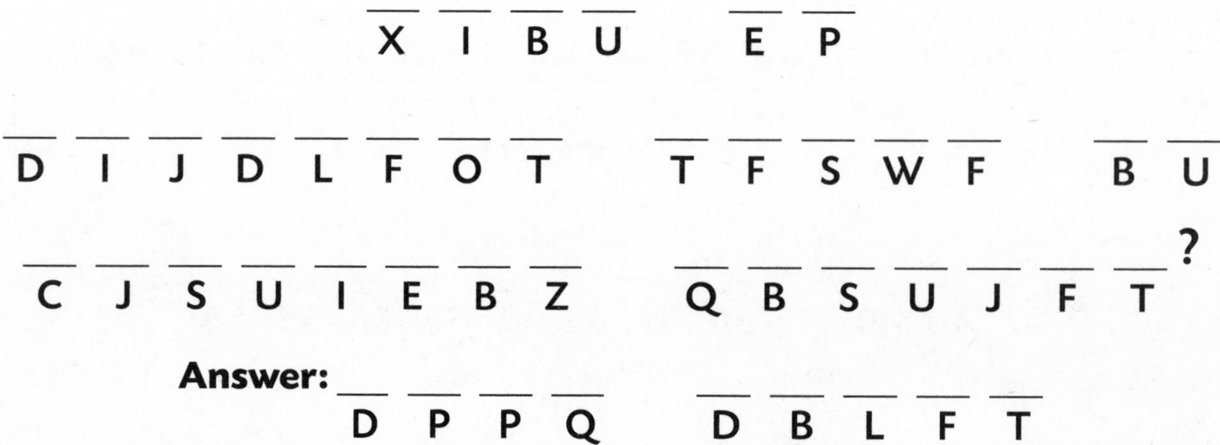

X I B U E P
D I J D L F O T T F S W F B U
C J S U I E B Z Q B S U J F T ?
Answer: D P P Q D B L F T

Hen Scratching

Each of these hens scratched a path in the dirt to her chick. Starting at the chicks, follow each line to find out which mother is at the end. Write the letters in the blanks.

1. ___ 2. ___ 3. ___ 4. ___ 5. ___

A B C D E

Around and Around

Write down EVERY OTHER letter as you go around the ring (you'll have to go around twice). The letters will spell out the answer to this riddle:

What happened after the chicken drank a bucket of cement?

START

I T D L E A W I A D L A K S I

URP!

cement

Answer: __ __   __ __ __ __ __

__   __ __ __ __ __ __ __ __ __

Finishing Line

Fill in the blanks to make words that fit the clues. Then read down to find a term for someone who's young.

This one sounds like a noise a bird makes.

The largest state in the USA	ALASKA
Popular board game	CHESS
Not costing a lot	CHEAP
The hottest season	SUMMER
City in Florida	MIAMA
Sour yellow fruit	LEMON
Make music	SING

And this one sounds like another word for cold.

Top floor of a house	ATTIC
Meal usually eaten at school	LUNCH
Spicy food made with meat and beans	CHILL
Flower with white or purple blossoms	LILAC
Place to keep money	BANK
The first number	ONE
Small red-breasted bird	ROBIN

Reading Material

Fill in each blank to make a word or phrase that names something to read. Then read down the column to answer this riddle:

What book gives you information about chickens?

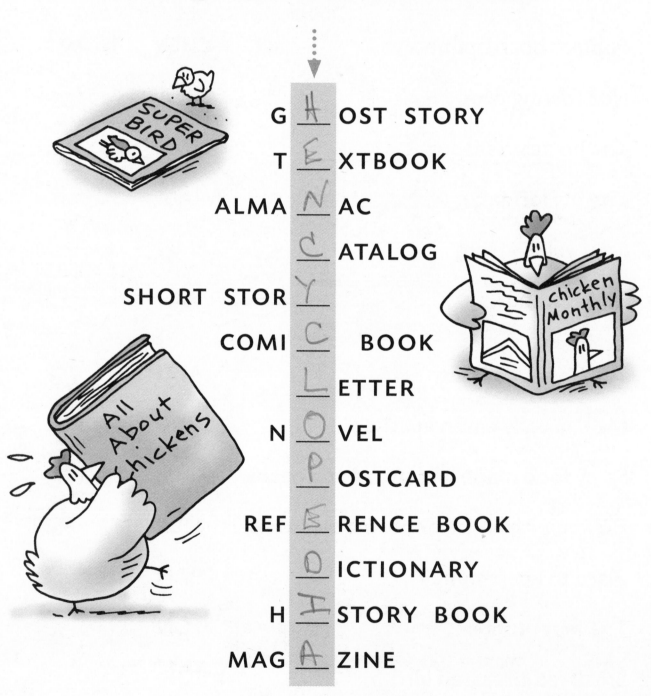

G __H__ OST STORY

T __E__ XTBOOK

ALMA __N__ AC

__C__ ATALOG

SHORT STOR __Y__

COMI __C__ BOOK

__L__ ETTER

N __O__ VEL

__P__ OSTCARD

REF __E__ RENCE BOOK

__D__ ICTIONARY

H __I__ STORY BOOK

MAG __A__ ZINE

Same Letters

An anagram is a word or phrase that uses the exact same letters to form another word or phrase. For example, FRESH TEA is an anagram of FEATHERS.

Can you match each chicken breed in the box with a silly phrase that's an anagram of it? But wait — there are two silly anagrams for each chicken breed! Find both and write the two letters in the blanks.

1. ___ ___ AUSTRALORP
2. ___ ___ BOOTED BANTAM
3. ___ ___ FAVEROLLE
4. ___ ___ LAKENVELDER
5. ___ ___ MODERN GAME
6. ___ ___ WYANDOTTE

A. LAVENDER ELK

B. FLEA LOVER

C. ATTEND BAMBOO

D. OGRE MADMEN

E. WENT TODAY

F. A RURAL SPOT

G. NABBED TOMATO

H. WANTED TOY

I. SALT UPROAR

J. EEL FLAVOR

K. ANGERED MOM

L. RANKED LEVEL

Yum!
Eel flavor!

Photo Match

Only one of these photos is exactly the same as the ORIGINAL. Which do you think it is?

ORIGINAL

1

2

3

4

5

A Cheese-y Puzzle

Most omelets contain cheese, 12 types of which are listed here. Place each one into its "eggs-act" spot in the grid. Start with the letters that are already in place and you will fill up the grid quickly.

4 Letters

BRIE
EDAM
FETA

5 Letters

SWISS

6 Letters

ROMANO

7 Letters

CHEDDAR
FONTINA
HAVARTI

8 Letters

AMERICAN
MUENSTER
PARMESAN

10 Letters

MOZZARELLA

R

B

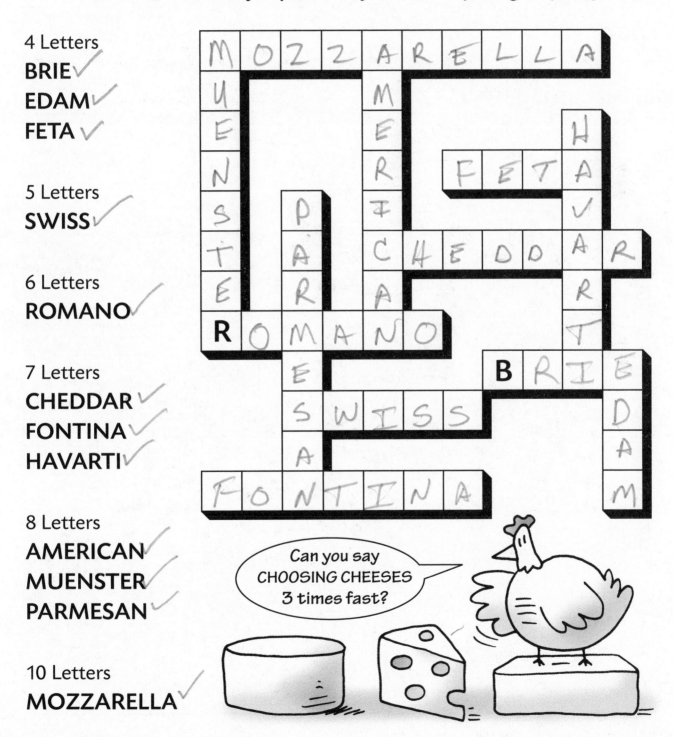

Can you say CHOOSING CHEESES 3 times fast?

Picture Pieces

Can you match the pieces on the next page to those in the drawing below? Just write the number and letter in the blank space above each piece. We've done the first to get you started.

1 2 3 4 5

A

B

C

D

E

F

A4

Doubles

Each word in the WORD BOX will answer one of the DOUBLE CLUES. Find that word and write it in the grid, making sure to put it on the correct line. We did the first one for you. When you're done, read down the gray column to find a two-word phrase that has two different meanings.

WORD BOX

BLUE	MOUSE
DOUGH	PITCHER
EARTH	~~TRUNK~~
KING	

One meaning of the phrase in the gray column is money saved for a major expense.

The other meaning is a fake item that a farmer uses to encourage hens to lay.

DOUBLE CLUES:

1. Large suitcase/part of a tree
2. Sad/color of the sky
3. Small rodent/device for a computer user
4. Player who throws a baseball/ Container for pouring liquids
5. The planet we live on/dirt
6. Father of a prince/chess piece
7. Floury mass used for baking/ another word for money

Remember

Study this picture for one minute, trying to memorize everything in it. Then turn the page and see if you can answer seven questions about it.

3

White Ribbon Winner

Ingredients
- Corn
- Barley
- Flowers

POULTRY FARMS

CHICKEN FEED

ONE POUND

(continued)

Read the previous page before looking at these questions.

1. What is the weight shown on the box?

____

2. How many chickens can you see on the box?

____

3. Has the box been opened?

____

4. Name any ingredient listed on the side of the box:

____

5. What animal other than a chicken appears on the box?

____

6. What color ribbon is on the side of the box?

____

7. How many trees are on the front of the box?

____

In Plain Sight

Every answer here is right in front of you. Cross out some letters from each chicken breed in the left column so that the remaining letters will spell a new word that answers the clue in the middle column. Do not change the order of the letters. The first one has been done to get you started.

Cross off:	Clue:	Answer:
1. AUSTRALORP	Part of a wristwatch	STRAP
2. DORKING	A collie or a poodle	DOGS
3. SUMATRA	Used a chair	SAT
4. PYNCHEON	Female chicken	HEN
5. ORPINGTON	Finger jewelry	RING
6. HOLLAND	The end of your arm	HAND
7. FAVEROLLE	Another word for autumn	FALL
8. CHANTECLER	Automobile	CAR
9. CAMPINE	A walking stick	CANE
10. BRAHMA	A male sheep	RAM
11.WYANDOTTE	Walk in shallow water	WADE
12.YOKOHAMA	Sweet potato	YAM
13. PHOENIX	Writing tool	PEN
14. HAMBURG	Large drinking cup	MUG

Food for Thought

Write a letter in each blank space to name things that are often fed to chickens. Then read down the column to name the part of a chicken's stomach that contains tiny stones used to grind up its food.

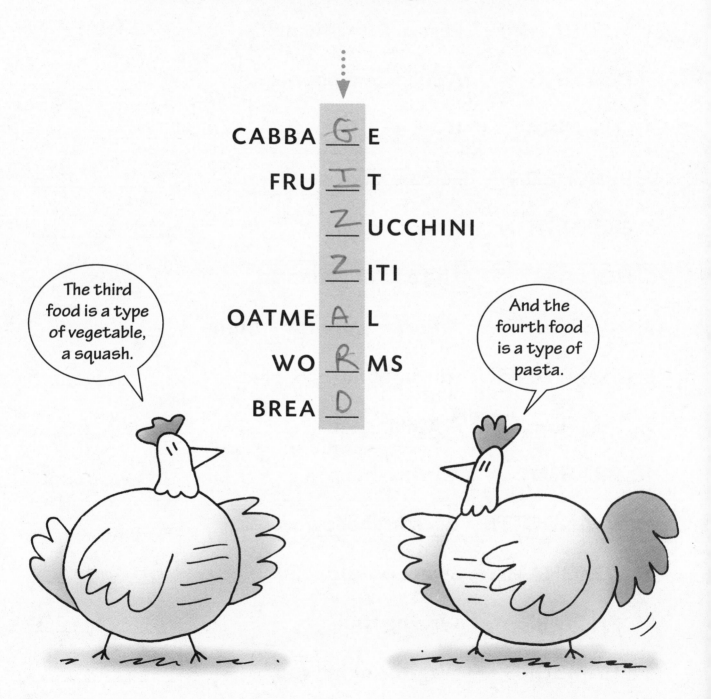

CABBA _G_ E

FRU _I_ T

_Z_ UCCHINI

_Z_ ITI

OATME _A_ L

WO _R_ MS

BREA _D_

The third food is a type of vegetable, a squash.

And the fourth food is a type of pasta.

State Bird

Put the names of 14 states into the grid in alphabetical order. Then read down the gray column to find the name of the state bird of Delaware.

WYOMING	GEORGIA
ALASKA	KENTUCKY
CONNECTICUT	HAWAII
MAINE	NEW MEXICO
SOUTH CAROLINA	ALABAMA
SOUTH DAKOTA	NEW HAMPSHIRE
VERMONT	MICHIGAN

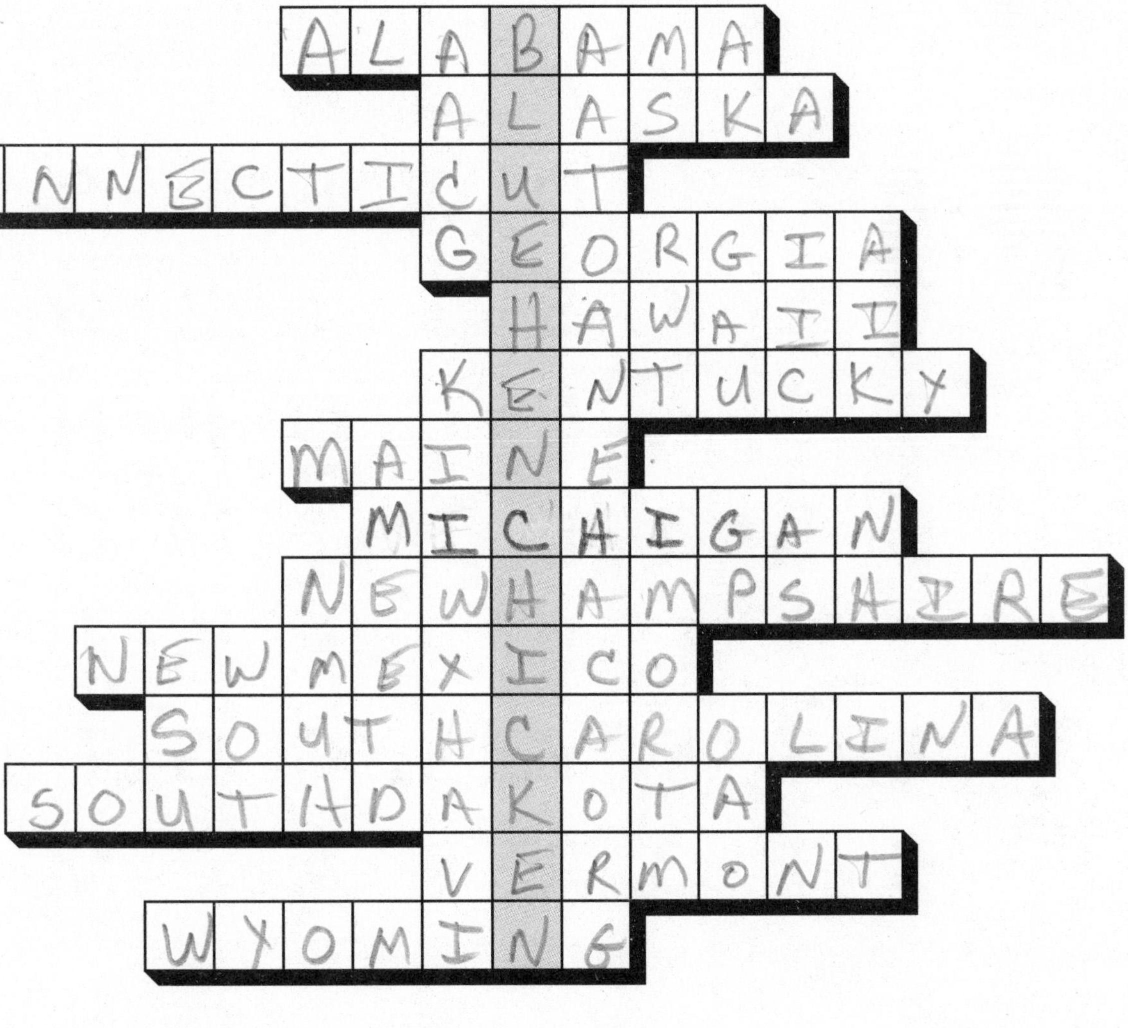

ALABAMA
ALASKA
CONNECTICUT
GEORGIA
HAWAII
KENTUCKY
MAINE
MICHIGAN
NEW HAMPSHIRE
NEW MEXICO
SOUTH CAROLINA
SOUTH DAKOTA
VERMONT
WYOMING

What a Treat!

The 13 words below are things that can be fed to chickens. Can you find and circle them in the grid? Look across, down, and diagonally (on a slant), both forward and backward. Circle each word when you find it, and cross it off the list.

Look for these words:

APPLES	EGGS	LETTUCE
CARROTS	FLOWERS	MELON
CEREAL	GRITS	MILK
CORN	KALE	ROLLS
CRICKETS		

L	R	L	A	E	R	E	C
E	F	L	O	W	E	R	S
T	L	S	S	T	I	R	G
T	Z	A	C	C	O	R	N
U	R	Q	K	L	I	M	O
C	S	E	L	P	P	A	L
E	T	S	Y	S	G	G	E
S	T	O	R	R	A	C	M

Cluckers

Match up the jokes and their answers by writing the letters in the blank spaces.

1. C What do young chickens get when they drink bubbly drinks too fast?
2. A What is a chicken's least favorite day?
3. E What do you find after eggs have hatched on the beach?
4. D What do you get when a hen lays an egg on a hill?
5. B A farmer has 10 eggs in each hand. If 10 more are added to each hand, what does he have?

A. FRY-DAY

B. REALLY BIG HANDS

C. THE CHICK-UPS

D. AN EGG ROLL

E. SEA SHELLS

Chicken Run

Put the point of your pencil in the first START box. Close your eyes and try to draw a line to the END box with the same number. Stop whenever you want, open your eyes and take a look. If your pencil point isn't inside the END box, close your eyes again and continue drawing from where you left off.

It counts as one point each time you open your eyes. Touching or crossing a gray wall also adds a point! The player with the fewest points wins.

Play all four games, alone or with a friend.

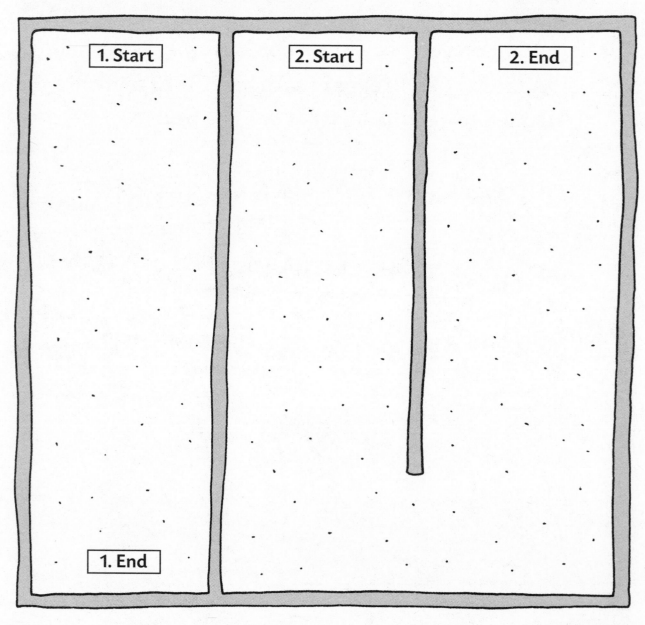

1. Start

2. Start

2. End

1. End

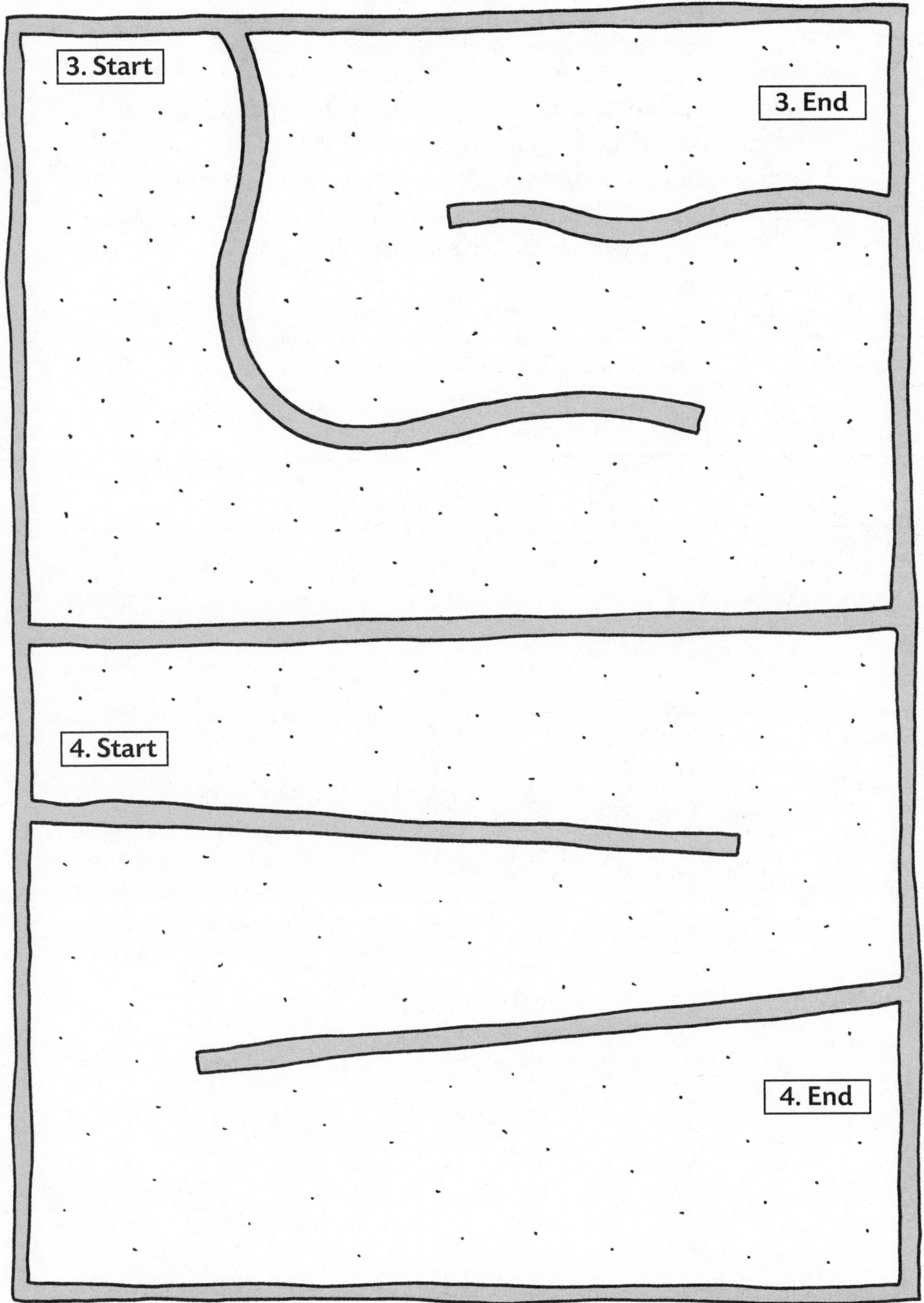
3. Start
3. End
4. Start
4. End

Step by Step

To find a riddle and its answer, start at the circled letter in the grid and move one square at a time. Move left, right, up, or down, but not diagonally (on a slant). Write each letter in the blank space when you find it, and cross it off in the grid. Each letter and symbol in the grid is used only once.

R	O	F	E	B	N	E	K	O	S	Y	L	A
E	I	T	I	S	U	S	E	R	B	A	W	S
.	G	G	E	N	A	?	D	(W)	H	A	T	I

Riddle: W __ __ __   __ __   __ __ __ __ __ __

__ __ __ __ __ __   __ __ __ __ __ __   __ __

__ __   __ __ __ __ ?

Riddle answer: __ __   __ __ __ .

The first letter in the *riddle answer* starts one square away from the "?" at the end of the riddle.

Be careful when you get to the K. An E is next, but which E?

DUSK

Time for Some Heavier Lifting

DIFFICULTY RATING:

3 Eggs

Wormholes

The worms are trying to find a way outside that avoids the hungry chickens. Can you find the one safe route?

End

Start

42

Hide and Seek

One dozen different chicken breeds are written in the box and also hidden in the sentences below. To find them, look at the letters at the end of one word and join them to the beginning of the next word. (Some terms are even hidden across three or four words.) Circle each word you find and cross it off the list like we did for ASEEL.

~~ASEEL~~	CORNISH	MINORCA	SEBRIGHT
BANDARA	MALAY	NANKIN	SERAMA
CAMPINE	MARANS	REDCAP	STAR

THEY WANTED TO CHASE ELEPHANTS.

THE CORN IS HIGH IN THE FIELD.

WHICH MINOR CAN PLAY BALL?

THEY READ THE LAST ARTICLE.

IS NAN KIND? YES.

SHE BOUGHT A RED CAPE.

THEY WENT TO CAMP IN ENGLAND.

OMAR ANSWERED ALL THE QUESTIONS.

TAKE A CAB AND A RAILROAD TO GET THERE.

IS THE ADVISER A MATH TEACHER?

THOSE BRIGHT KIDS GOT GREAT MARKS.

IN GUATEMALA YOUNG PEOPLE PLAY SOCCER.

Who wanted to chase elephants?!

Not me!

Part Time

All the words in these two drawings are scrambled (the letters are in the wrong order). Using the list at the top of the next page, write the unscrambled chicken part in each space. Cover up the list for an extra challenge.

KABE: Beak

ELDADS: Saddle

HINCOUS: cushion

LEWTAT: wattle

GWIN: Wing

KOCH: Hoch

KNASH: Shank

OTE: Toe

Unscrambled Words

BEAK BREAST CAPE COMB CUSHION
FLUFF HOCK SADDLE SHANK SICKLES
SPUR THIGH TOE WATTLE WING

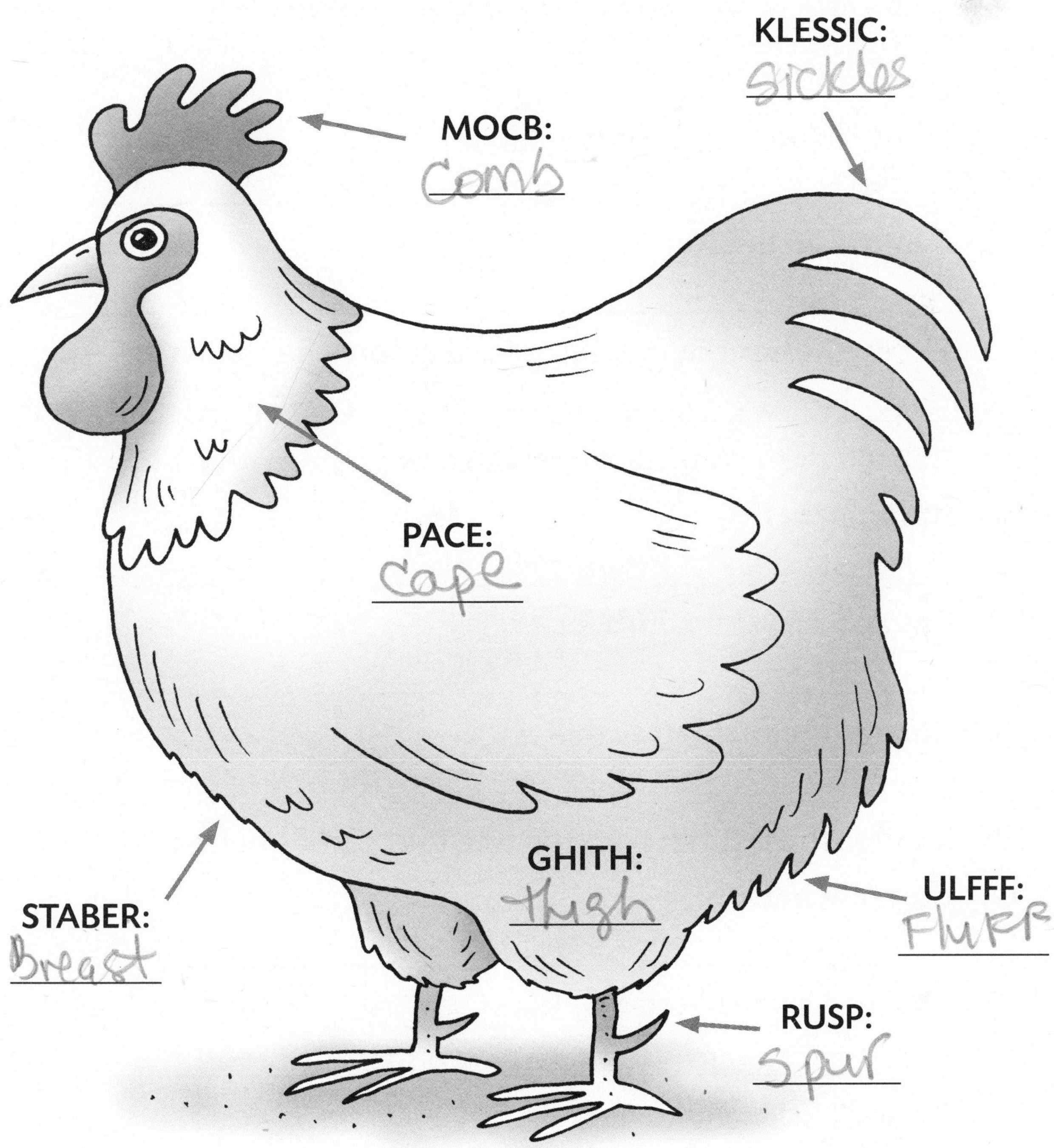

Following Directions

Follow the directions below LINE BY LINE.
Write the letters carefully on the blanks and you'll change CATALANA (a chicken breed) to another chicken breed.

1. Write the word CATALANA:

   ____

2. Remove all the A's:

   ____

3. Put an O after the first letter and before the last letter:

   ____

4. Change the T to the letter that comes before it in it in the alphabet:

   ____

5. Put an E after the third letter:

   ____

6. Change the first letter to R :

   ____

7. Change the last letter to the one that comes before it in the alphabet:

   ____

8. Change the fifth letter to C:

   ____

9. Put a B at the end:

   ____

Egg Collecting 2

Players take turns. On each turn, draw a short line to connect two dots. When a triangle is completed, surrounding an egg, mark your initials on that egg. The player who collects (initials) the most eggs wins.

Talking Turkey

Rudy and Buttercup's turkey pal, Gobbler, has come for a visit. And he's brought along some friends. Using the clues below, can you figure out which turkey is Gobbler?

Gobbler…

…has four tail feathers
…isn't sitting down
…has a snood (that thing hanging over his beak)
…has a body bigger than a bowling ball
…is wearing a hat
…isn't looking at his tail
…isn't flying

Name that Place

Put one of the 3-letter names in each set of blanks to form a word that answers the clue. Then move the numbered letters to the same numbered blanks at the bottom to find the name of a real place in Pennyslvania.

ACE ART CAL EVA HAL IDA
IKE LEO RON VAN WES

Clue	Word
A show with singing and dancing	MUSI ___(1) ___ ___
Disappear	___ ___ ___(7) ISH
Highway	TURNP ___ ___(5) ___
Home for royalty	PAL ___ ___(4) ___
Moving "cage" in a building	EL ___(6) ___ ___ TOR
50 percent	___(2) ___ ___ F
Our planet	E ___ ___ ___(8) H
U.S. region where Arizona is located	SOUTH ___(10) ___ ___ T
Powerful	ST ___ ___ ___(11) G
The "Sunshine State"	FLOR ___(3) ___ ___
Large animal with black spots	___ ___ ___(9) PARD

Answer: ___ ___ ___ ___ ___ ___ ___ ___ ___ ___ ___
1 2 3 4 5 6 7 8 9 10 11

Free-Range Fun

There are 8 differences between the drawing below and the one on the next page. Circle each one as you find it.

Isn't it great to be free?
No. I like costing a lot of money.
HI, WOW

More Riddle Fun

Write the answer to each clue in the numbered blanks. Then move each letter to the same-numbered space in the box on the next page. Work back and forth between the clues and the box to find a riddle and its answer.

New York... ___ ___ ___ ___
10 14 25 3

Carry groceries in this: ___ ___ ___
32 30 16

A bird that quacks: ___ ___ ___ ___
6 18 34 48

Put words on paper: ___ ___ ___ ___ ___
1 21 5 7 27

People from the Netherlands: ___ ___ ___ ___ ___
4 36 45 57 52

Moves through water in a pool: ___ ___ ___ ___ ___
23 41 39 19 44

A person who educates: ___ ___ ___ ___ ___ ___ ___
40 12 35 54 26 9 28

___ and tell (kindergarten activity): ___ ___ ___ ___
24 55 22 13

One quarter (a coin) is 25... ___ ___ ___ ___ ___
20 53 60 49 37

The U.S. president lives in the White... ___ ___ ___ ___ ___
2 29 46 43 59

Here's another clue for this one.

Some Amish, Brethren, and Mennonites are Pennsylvania _____.

Birthday party treat with candles: ___ ___ ___ ___
47 42 58 38

Over; finished: ___ ___ ___ ___
31 50 15 33

The top part of your leg: ___ ___ ___ ___ ___
51 8 56 17 11

Riddle:

___ ___ ___   ___ ___ ___   ___ ___ ___
1 2 3   4 5 6   7 8 9

___ ___ ___ ___ ___ ___ ___   ___ ___ ___
10 11 12 13 14 15 16   17 18 19

___ ___ ___ ___ ___   ___ ___ ___   ___ ___ ___ ___ ?
20 21 22 23 24   25 26 27   28 29 30 31

Riddle answer:

___ ___ ___ ___ ___ ___ ___   ___ ___   ___ ___ ___
32 33 34 35 36 37 38   39 40   41 42 43

___ ___ ___ ___ ___   ___ ___   ___ ___ ___
44 45 46 47 48   49 50   51 52 53

___ ___ ___ ___ ___ ___ ___ .
54 55 56 57 58 59 60

Scaredy Cat

Nine words or phrases meaning AFRAID are hidden in the grid. Look forward, backward, up, down, and diagonally (on a slant) for each one. Circle each item when you find it. Reading from left to right and top to bottom, put the UNCIRCLED letters in the blanks to find a word that means "fear of chickens."

Look for these words:

FEARFUL
FIDGETY
JUMPY
ON EDGE
SCARED
SKITTISH
STARTLED
TENSE
UNEASY

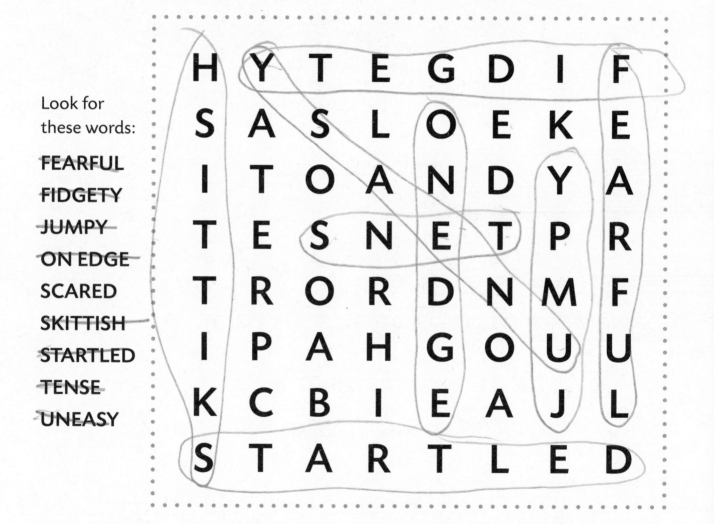

H	Y	T	E	G	D	I	F
S	A	S	L	O	E	K	E
I	T	O	A	N	D	Y	A
T	E	S	N	E	T	P	R
T	R	O	R	D	N	M	F
I	P	A	H	G	O	U	U
K	C	B	I	E	A	J	L
S	T	A	R	T	L	E	D

Answer: __ __ __ __ __ __ __ __ __ __ __ __ __ __

Be afraid. Be very afraid.
Not!

50

Imagine It

Remembering a list of words is sometimes easier if you create a funny picture in your mind. For example, try to memorize the first list below by picturing a CHICKEN with PAIL on its head. On the pail is an EGG with a PENCIL sticking out of it, and so on.

Finish creating a mental picture of the first list and, when you're ready, turn the page to see if you can write the words in order. Then come back here and do the same thing for the second list.

1

CHICKEN
PAIL
EGG
PENCIL
ROPE
APPLE
WATER
FROG
(8 words)

2

HEN HOUSE
FLAG
SPIDER
SHOVEL
KITE
GOOSE
SNEEZE
CLOUD
LADDER
FARMER
(10 words)

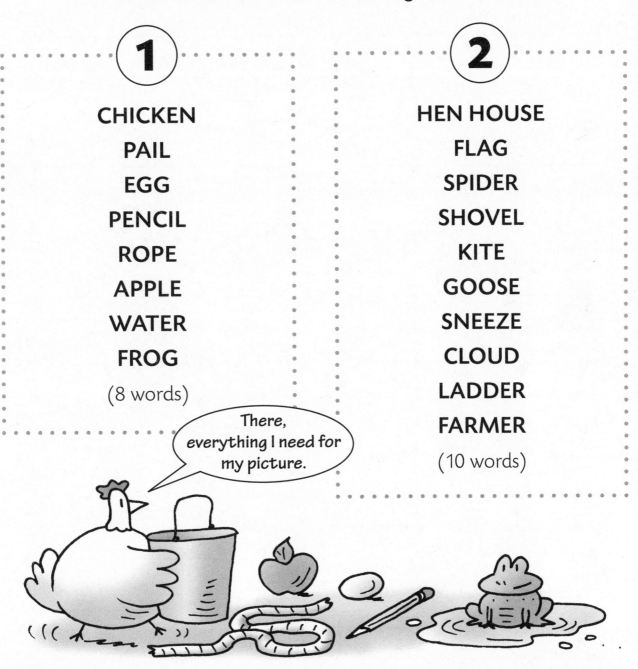

There, everything I need for my picture.

Imagine It

Follow the instructions on the previous page, then come back here and fill in the blanks.

1

____

____

____

____

____

____

____

____

2

____

____

____

____

____

____

____

____

____

____

Make up your own lists.

Use verbs and adjectives to make it harder.

Farm Walk

Buttercup needs to collect six white eggs, one from each nest, and then put them in her basket. Rudy needs to do likewise, picking up six brown eggs (they're gray in the drawing) and put them in his basket.

Just one catch – once Buttercup visits a nest, she can't come back to it again! The same for Rudy (but he *can* visit nests Buttercup has visited). Starting in the direction each is headed, can you find both routes?

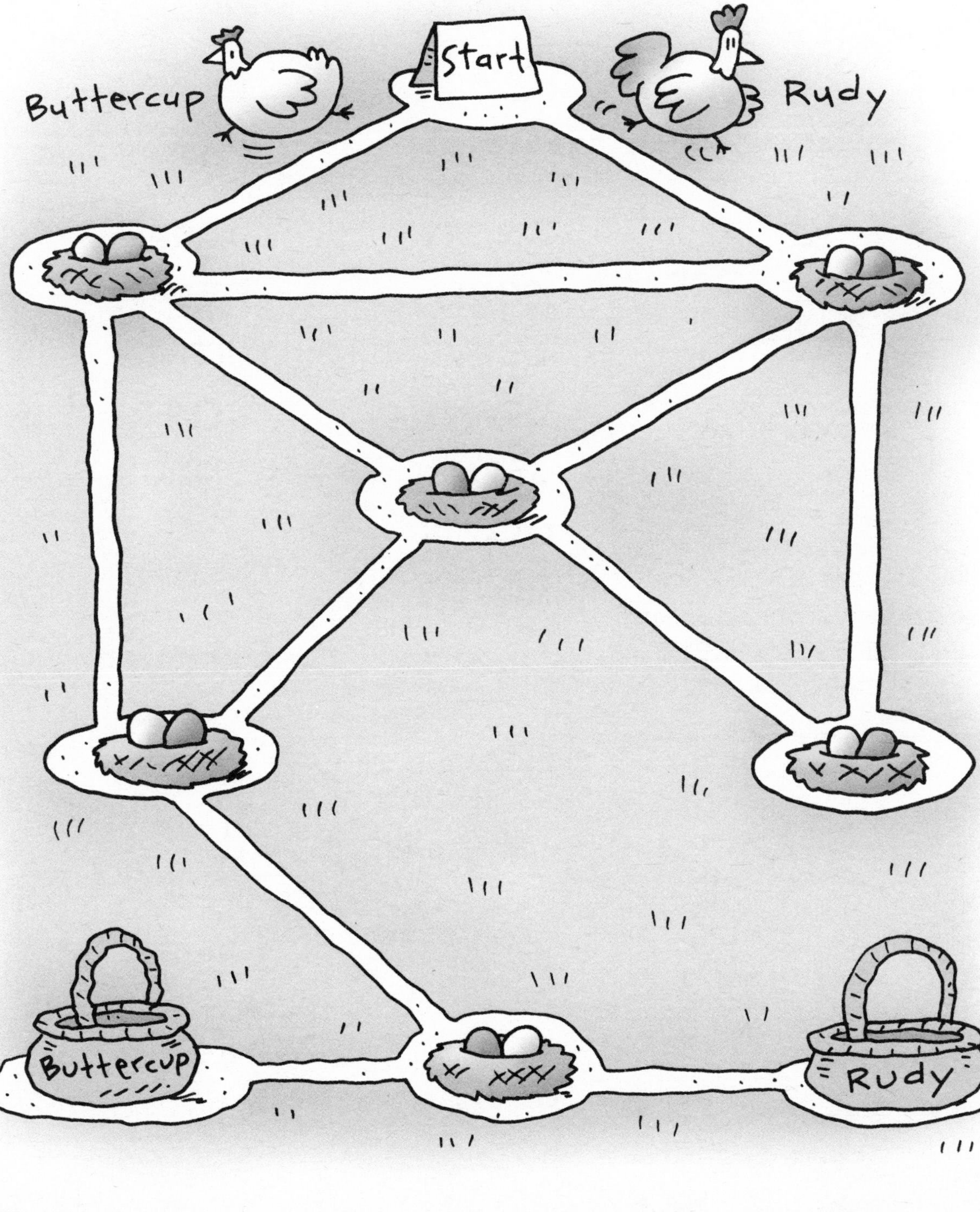

Start

Buttercup

Rudy

Buttercup

Rudy

Double Trouble

The word list below contains seven words formed by using only the letters in JERSEY GIANT (a chicken breed) and eight words formed by using only the letters in CREVECOEUR (another breed).

Each word fits into only one of the grids. To figure out which ones go where, start with the letters that have been filled in already. Cross off each word after you write it in the grid.

3 Letters

OUR

4 Letters

EVER

5 Letters

ANGRY
CORER
CURVE
GRANT
JEANS
OCCUR
ROVER

6 Letters

AGREES
GREASE
JITNEY
REVERE
STRAIN

7 Letters

RECOVER

Hey, all the letters in JERSEY GIANT can be rearranged to spell "IT'S JEAN GREY."

And CREVECOEUR can spell "RECOVER CUE."

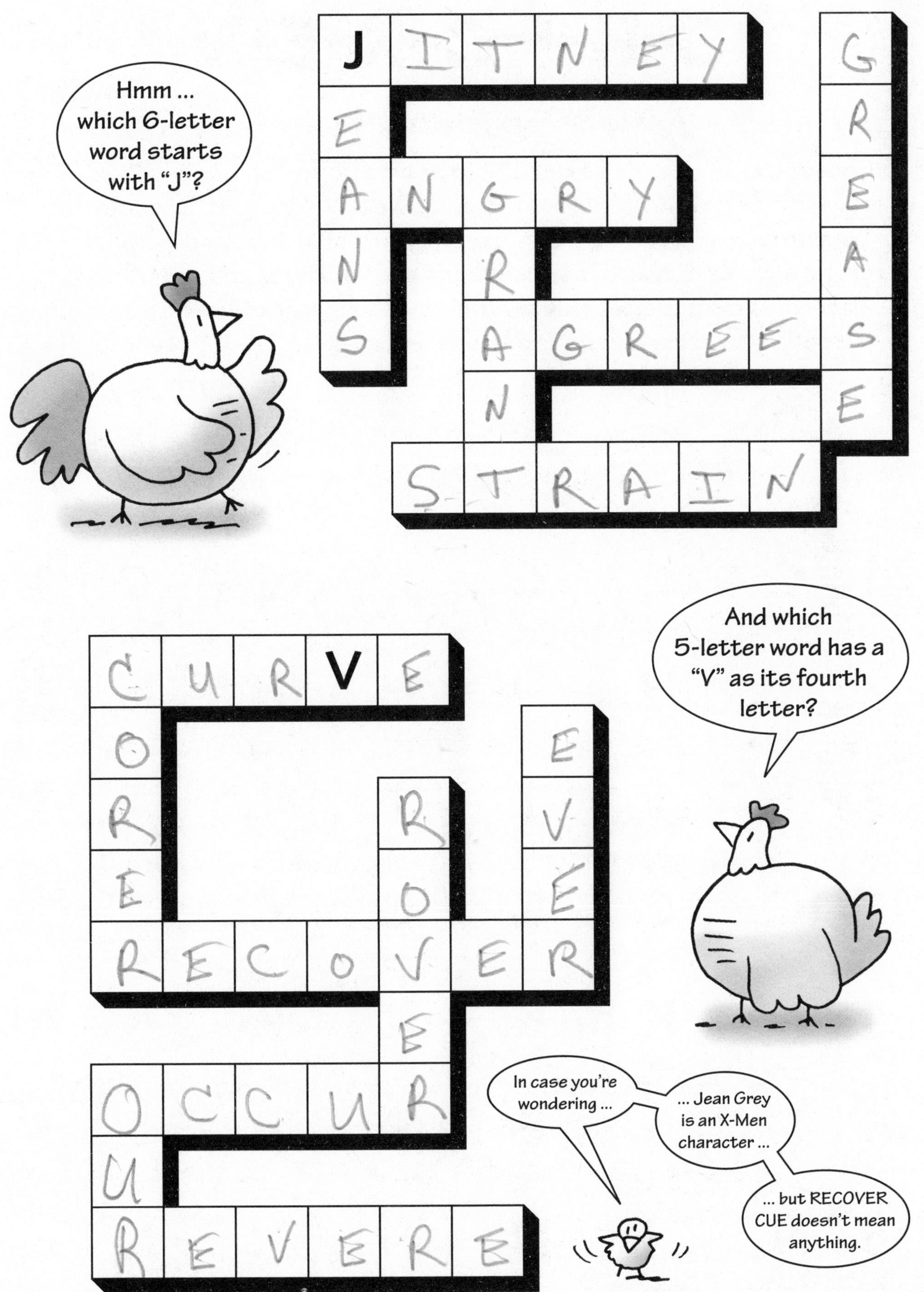
J
Hmm ... which 6-letter word starts with "J"?
V
And which 5-letter word has a "V" as its fourth letter?
In case you're wondering ...
... Jean Grey is an X-Men character ...
... but RECOVER CUE doesn't mean anything.

C-H-I-C-K-E-N

A game for 1 to 6 players using one die.

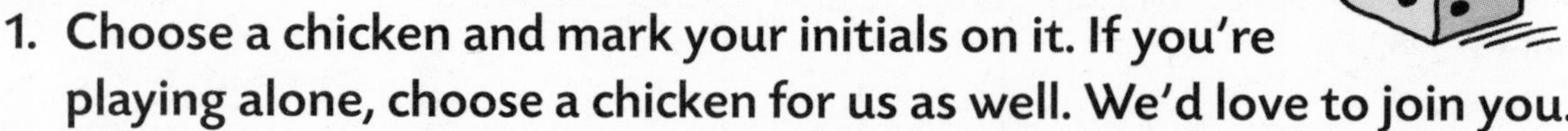

1. Choose a chicken and mark your initials on it. If you're playing alone, choose a chicken for us as well. We'd love to join you.
2. Take turns rolling the die (roll for us). If your roll is 1, cross off one of the two "C" circles. If it's 2, cross off the "H" circle, and so on.
3. Players cross off a letter only for their own rolls, not someone else's.
4. First player to cross off all their letters and spell C-H-I-C-K-E-N wins.

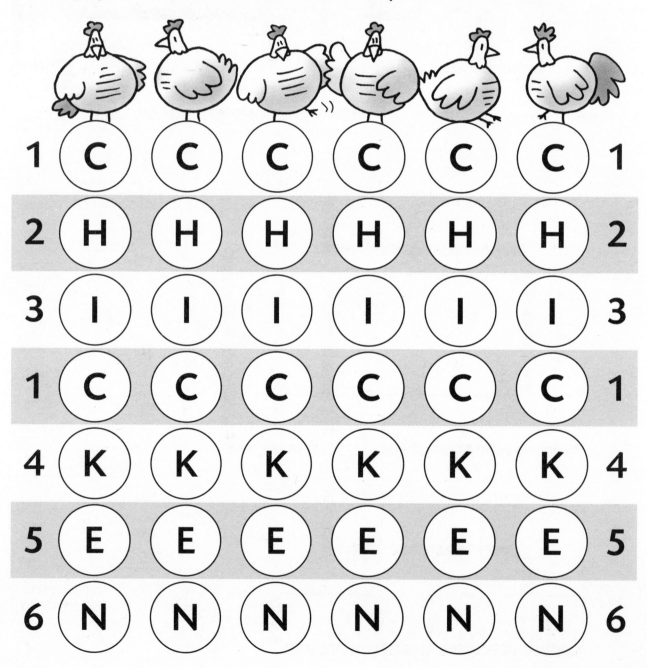

1	C	C	C	C	C	C	1
2	H	H	H	H	H	H	2
3	I	I	I	I	I	I	3
1	C	C	C	C	C	C	1
4	K	K	K	K	K	K	4
5	E	E	E	E	E	E	5
6	N	N	N	N	N	N	6

The Hen Zone

Put the letters H-E-N (in any order) in the blanks to form a word that answers each clue.

Clue	Answer
12 of these equal one foot	I N C H E S
A sweetener made by bees	H O N E Y
Truthful, like Abe Lincoln	H O N E S T
The number after 17	E I G G T E E N
Filled with ghosts, like a Halloween house	H A U N T E D
A wild animal that makes a laughing sound	H Y E N A
At what time?	W H E N
___ checkers (board game)	C H I N E S E
Opposite of southern	N O R T R E R N
Give light, like the sun	S H I N E
Reduce the length of a dress	S H O R T E N
Scare	F R I G H T E N

Express Yourself

In each word pair find the one letter in the LEFT word that is not in the RIGHT word and write in on the blank. Then read down to find a chicken-related term that means:

to run off or escape

FLOWERS	F	SLOWER
LICENSE	L	NIECES
YEARNED	Y	NEARED
STAPLER	T	PEARLS
PHRASES	H	SPARES
REPLACE	E	PARCEL
RICHEST	C	THEIRS
STOOPED	O	POSTED
TENSION	O	TENNIS
SPINACH	P	CHAINS

Yay! Another one.

Do the same thing here to find another chicken-related term that means:

to be in control, especially at home

MARBLES	R	BLAMES
DETOURS	U	STORED
CENTRAL	L	NECTAR
OUTSIDE	E	STUDIO
ANTLERS	T	LEARNS
WHIRLED	H	WILDER
ESSENCE	E	SCENES
TERRACE	R	CREATE
COASTER	O	REACTS
GROANED	O	GARDEN
ACTRESS	S	CRATES
TRACTOR	T	CARROT

Who Am I?

Your job is to find the breed of chicken described below.

Take each of the CAPITALIZED words in the description and place it in the grid, reading across. Use the letters that are already in place to guide you. Be sure to count the number of letters in each word to see if they'll fit.

When all the words are in place, read down the gray column to find the breed.

I'm an ENDANGERED breed from CHINA. My EGGS are medium to dark BROWN. I need SHELTER when the WEATHER is too warm or too cold. I have a SINGLE comb. I'm one of the TALLEST birds.

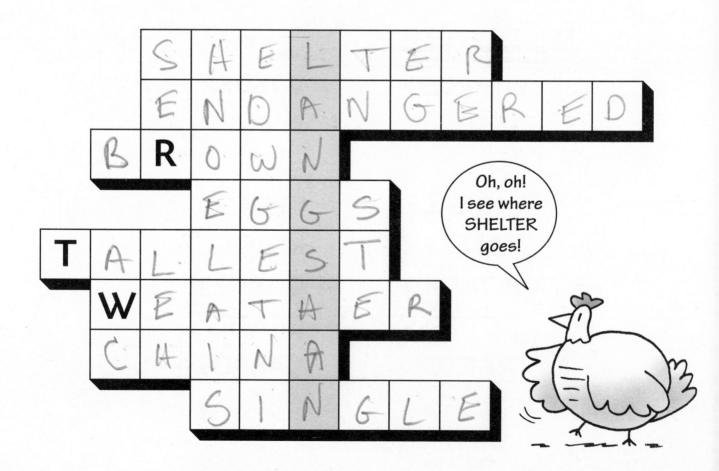

		R									
T											
	W										

Oh, oh!
I see where
SHELTER
goes!

I feel so smart figuring out where SMART goes. Hee hee.

Do the same thing again to find another breed.

I'm a rare BREED from HOLLAND whose ROOSTER is PICTURED on a FAMOUS box of CEREAL. My hens lay reddish BROWN eggs that are sometimes SPECKLED. I'm a SMART bird who loves to range freely.

			P						
						A			
				M					
							S		
						E			

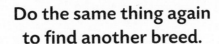

Funky Chicken

The chickens at this hoedown (a square dance) are doing a dance from the 1960s called the Funky Chicken. But only two of them are doing it exactly the same way. Can you pick out those two?

1.

2.

3.

4.

5.

6.

7.

8.

4

NIGHT

Come Home to Roost— and Solve

DIFFICULTY RATING:

4 Eggs

57

Before or After

Change each letter to the one that comes either BEFORE or AFTER it in the alphabet. Example: X could be W or Y. Choose the correct letters to find a riddle and its answer.

Here is a copy of the alphabet to help you:

A B C D E F G H I J K L M N O P Q R S T U V W X Y Z

Riddle:

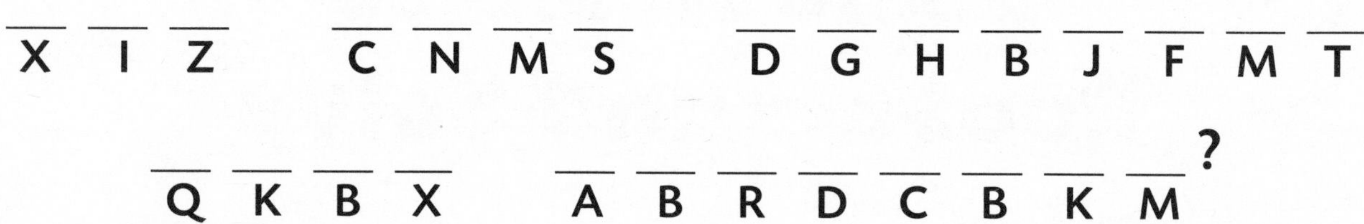

__ __ __   __ __ __ ' __   __ __ __ __ __ __ __ __

X I Z   C N M S   D G H B J F M T

__ __ __ __   __ __ __ __ __ __ __ __ ?

Q K B X   A B R D C B K M

Answer:

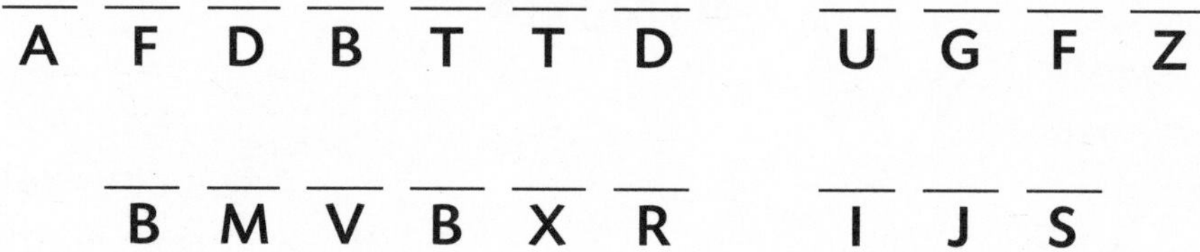

A F D B T T D   U G F Z

B M V B X R   I J S

G P X K   C B M K R .

Wait, I don't get it.
It's a play on words — FOWL, as in chickens, and FOUL, a baseball hit outside the lines.

Chicken Wire

The wires in this piece of fencing have been cut so that there's only one way to get through from START to END. Can you find it?

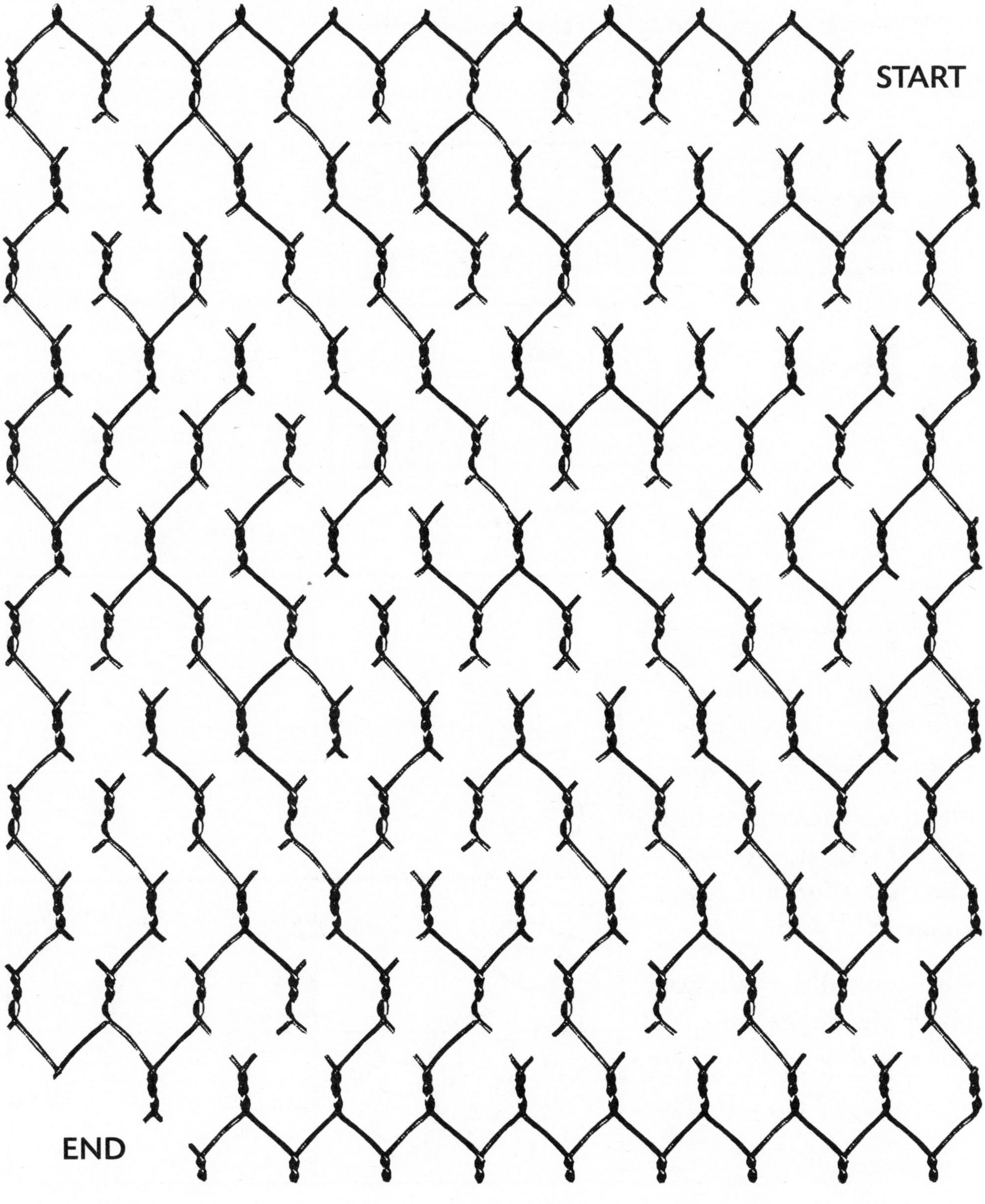

START

END

59

Chicken Sudoku

Fill in the boxes using these four different drawings: Each drawing must appear ONCE in each row going across, ONCE in each column going down, and ONCE in each 4-square box (with the heavier outlines).

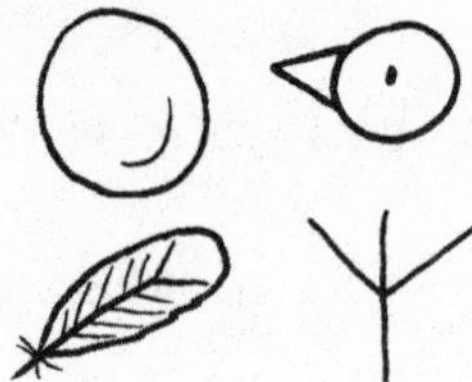

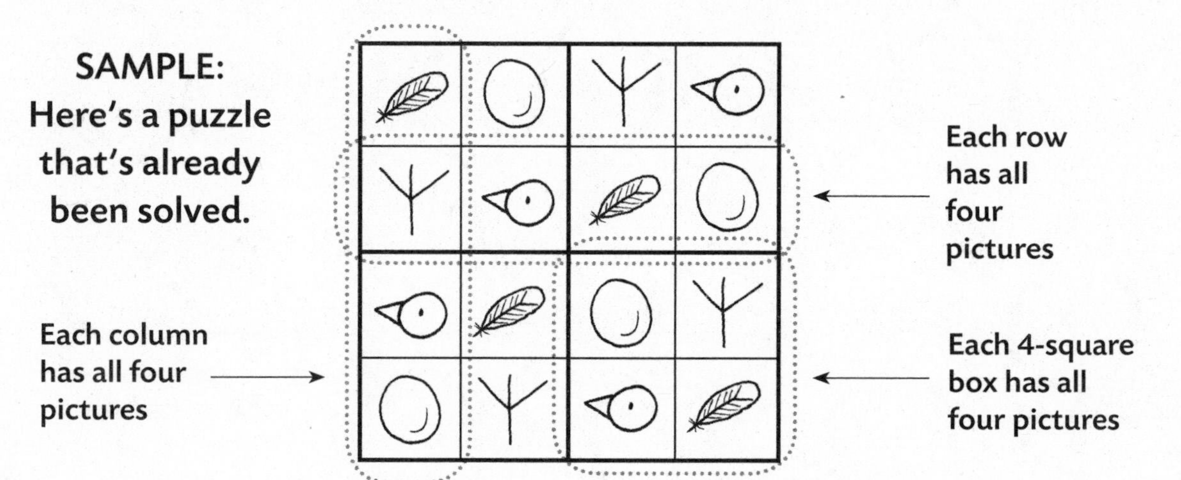
SAMPLE:
Here's a puzzle that's already been solved.
Each row has all four pictures
Each column has all four pictures
Each 4-square box has all four pictures

1.

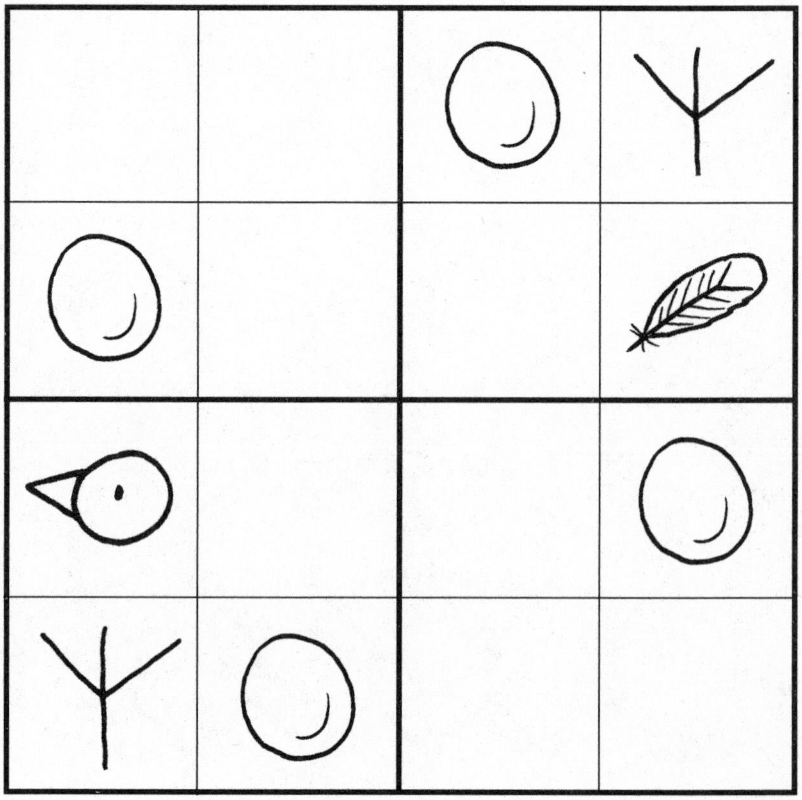

HINTS:

Start with the upper left square. There's only one choice, the feather.

Next, look across the top row. There's now only one choice for the second square.

Also, look at the 4-square box in the upper right. Just one drawing missing there.

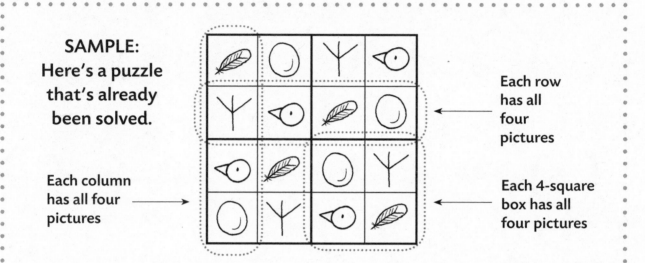

2.
I'm going to start with the top row here.
Yikes! Just four drawings to start with?
3.

There are just two blank squares across the top. Use the drawings in the squares right below those two to help you figure out what goes in them.

Start with the two middle columns. Then work from there. No guessing is needed – keep looking and you'll always find a square you'll know for sure.

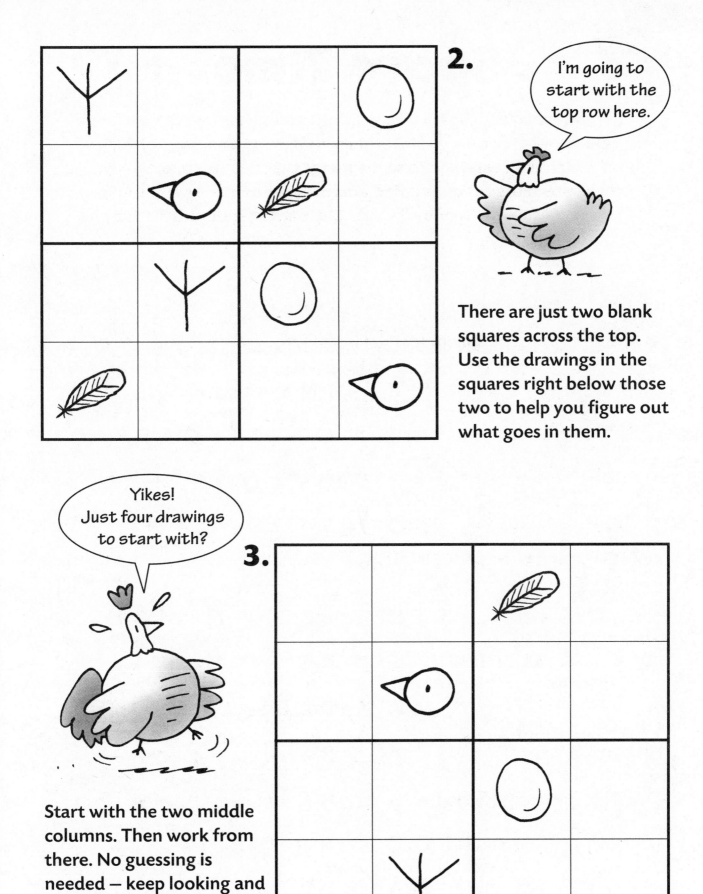

Spare Time

Do you spend your spare time playing games, reading, or watching television? Or, do you collect things that are special to you? Fill in the blanks on each line to name things that people collect. Then read down the column to find a term that describes people who raise chickens in their backyards (the ones who do this for fun).

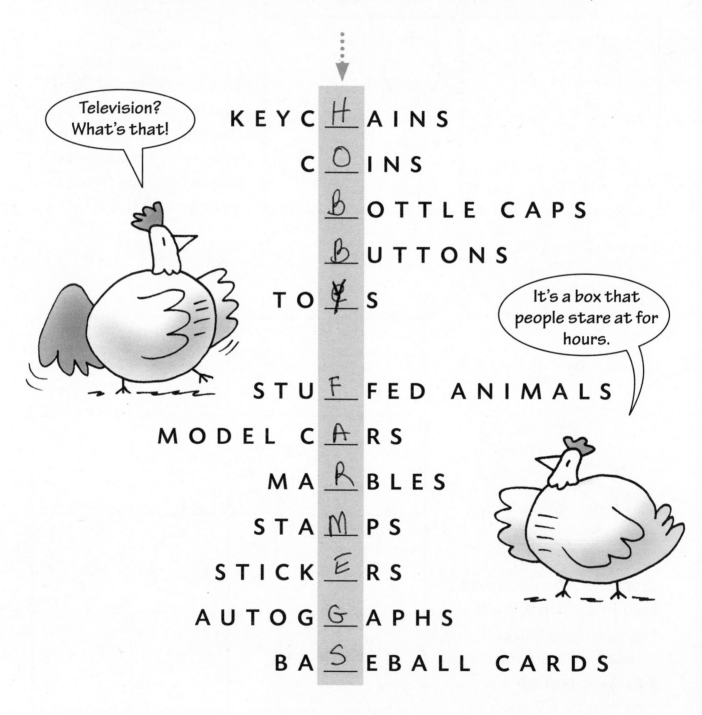

Television? What's that!

KEYC H AINS

C O INS

B OTTLE CAPS

B UTTONS

TO Y S

STU F FED ANIMALS

MODEL C A RS

MA R BLES

STA M PS

STICK E RS

AUTOG G APHS

BA S EBALL CARDS

It's a box that people stare at for hours.

Comb Over

Make chicken combs for you and a friend to wear on top of your heads.

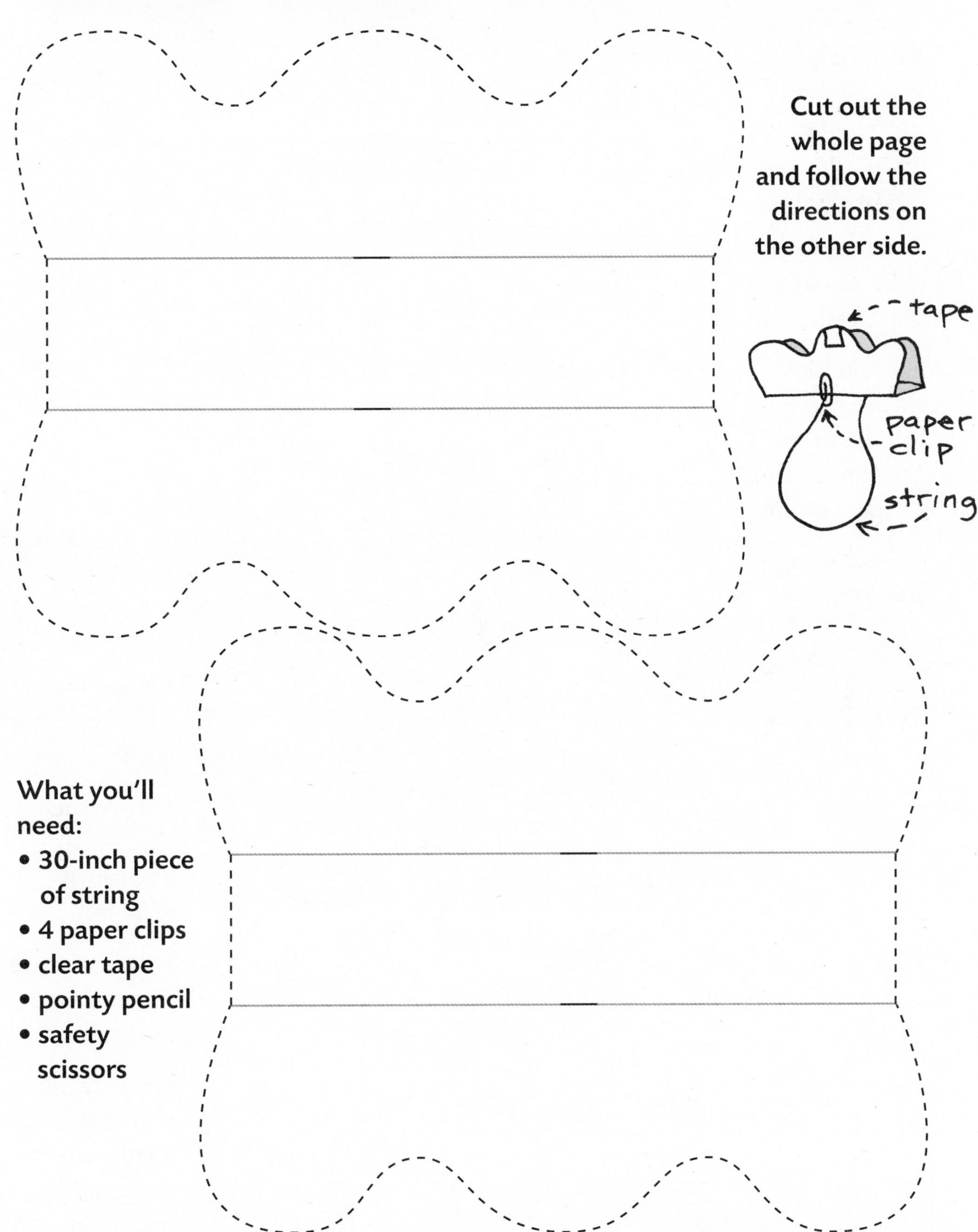

Cut out the whole page and follow the directions on the other side.

What you'll need:

- 30-inch piece of string
- 4 paper clips
- clear tape
- pointy pencil
- safety scissors

ACTIVITY

Comb Over

(See previous page)

1. Have an adult help you cut out both pieces along the dotted lines.
2. Color both sides of each piece red.
3. Make tiny slits in the middle of the gray lines using a pencil point.
4. Fold along the gray lines.
5. Tape the sides together at the very top.
6. Tie paper clips on to both ends of string.
7. Attach paper clips to sides using slits.
8. Put comb on top of your head with the string under your chin.

Globe Trotting

Eighteen terms related to travel are hidden in the grid. Look forward, backward, up, down, and diagonally (on a slant) in all directions. Circle each item when you find it. Reading from left to right and top to bottom, put the UNCIRCLED letters into the blanks to find the answer to this riddle:

What do you call an egg that goes on a safari?

AIRPLANE
CAR
CRUISE
EXCURSION
GUIDE
HOTEL
INN
LUGGAGE
PASSPORT
RESORT
ROUTE
STATION
TOUR BUS
TRAIN
TRIP
VACATION
VISA
VOYAGE

Answer: AN EGGS-PLORER

Get Rid of It

Read each clue below and cross off its answer in the box on the next page. Then read the LEFTOVER words in that box, starting at the bottom right and going from right to left and bottom to top, and write them on the lines.

They won't make sense. But, after you change the first letter in each word, you'll find the answer to this riddle:

Why did the chicken cross the ocean?

1. Sound made by a chicken
2. Small amount of time
3. Well-mannered
4. In a bad mood
5. Perspire
6. Person who lives nearby
7. Quiet
8. Physical activity
9. Small insect
10. Walk slowly
11. Skinny
12. Rarely
13. Section of a book
14. Easily broken

WIDE	POLITE	CLUCK	ETHER
SILENT	THIN	EXERCISE	SHE
CHAPTER	SWEAT	NEIGHBOR	GRUMPY
INSTANT	SO	ANT	STROLL
BET	SELDOM	FRAGILE	NO

Leftover words:

____

____

____

____

____

____

Now change the first letter in each leftover word:

____

____

____

____

____

____

Be careful. Don't change the first letter of that last word to an "S."

Think of the word "ocean" to come up with the right answer.

True/False

Read each sentence and determine if it's TRUE or FALSE. If it's true, circle the letter in the true column; if it's false, circle the letter in the false column.

When you're done, write the circled letters on the same-numbered dashes below to discover the name of a chicken that lived to be 16 years old.

	True	False
1. Chickens are birds.	I	E
2. Fear of chickens is called insomnia.	G	D
3. Chickens fly south in the winter.	P	T
4. All chickens lay white eggs.	R	M
5. People who "walk on eggshells" are trying hard not to upset anyone.	A	U
6. An egg white omelet contains one yolk.	F	L
7. Free-range chickens are cooped up all the time.	O	A

Answer:

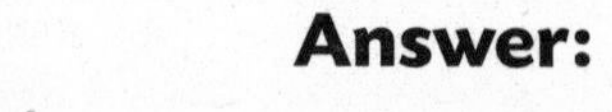

4 7 3 1 6 2 5

Oh! Oh!
I know that
first one!

Chicken Coupe

Some changes were made to Buttercup's new coupe (sports car). Things were removed, one item at a time. Can you put the pictures in order, starting with the way her car started out (with everything on it) and finishing with the way it ended up (with fewer things)? Write numbers in the blanks from 1 to 8.

A. _____

E. _____

B. _____

F. _____

C. _____

G. _____

D. _____

H. _____

Sicilian Buttercup

Sicilian Buttercup is a very rare breed of chicken from the island of Sicily. All the words below are spelled using the letters in SICILIAN BUTTERCUP.

Can you put each word into the grid on the next page? Start with the letters that are already in place, and you will fill up the grid quickly.

3 Letters

LET
TEN
USE

4 Letters

AUNT
CLUB
LATE
NEST
SUIT
TEAR

5 Letters

BRAIN
BURST
CENTS
CRUST
LASER
PETAL
SPACE

6 Letters

CIRCUS
INSECT
STRIPE

7 Letters

PLASTIC
SPECIAL

8 Letters

ARTICLES
PECULIAR

Look at that! A breed named after me!

You're famous, Buttercup! Take a bow.

This one is a little tricky, Buttercup.
We'll get it if we keep at it, Rudy!

Egg Match

There are 23 eggs below. Ten of them have an exact match, but three don't. Cross off the matched pairs to find the three oddballs . . . er, odd eggs.

Rare Breed

Put one letter into the blank space on each line to name an ordinary nine-letter word. Then read down the gray column to find a not-so-ordinary breed of chicken.

The first answer is a school subject where students study Earth and its features.

GEOG ___ APHY

HAMB ___ RGER

CLAS ___ ICAL

ADMI ___ SION

CONT ___ NENT

QUOT ___ TION

ADVE ___ TURE

CUST ___ DIAN

ENTE ___ TAIN

BUMB ___ EBEE

HARM ___ NICA

BRIE ___ CASE

SNOW ___ LAKE

The one starting with "CUST" is a person who keeps a school clean.

Missing in Action

Each chicken breed is missing some letters from its name. Take a word from the box and write its letters, in order, in the blanks to complete each breed's name. Each word is used once.

AND	CAMP	CAT	COMB
ELDER	EYE	HAM	HORN
KING	LAND	MAT	SUMMER

BARNEV _ _ _ _ _

BUCK _ _ _

RHODE IS _ _ _ _ RED

_ _ _ ALANA

ROSE _ _ _ _

_ _ _ ALUSIAN

DOR _ _ _ _

_ _ _ _ INE

_ _ _ BURG

LEG _ _ _ _

SU _ _ _ RA

WEL _ _ _ _ _ _

Counting the number of blanks helps.

That last one is the only one with six blanks.

Oh, goody, another one of these!

Do the same thing again to complete one dozen more chicken breeds.

ANT	AWARE	BRIGHT	CAP
CHANT	CORN	HIRE	HOE
LAKE	MOUTH	PIN	ROLL

_ _ _ _ _ECLER

P_ _ _NIX

SE_ _ _ _ _ _

RED_ _ _

OR_ _ _GTON

PLY_ _ _ _ _ ROCK

JERSEY GI_ _ _

FAVE_ _ _ _E

_ _ _ _NVELDER

NEW HAMPS_ _ _ _ RED

DEL_ _ _ _ _

_ _ _ _ISH

Only one answer with six blanks over here, too. I'm starting with that one.

Close Relatives

Change the underlined letter in each word to find four related words or phrases in each group. Write your new words on the lines. Rudy and Buttercup did the first one for you.

Materials for building chicken coops:

SAILS ____NAILS____

NUMBER ____________

THICKEN DIRE ____________

ROOTING ____________

Tools for building chicken coops:

HUMMER ____________

TOWER GRILL ____________

JAW ____________

RUDER ____________

Egg colors:

GLUE–GREEK ____________

DREAMY WHINE ____________

PARK CROWN ____________

SPACKLED ____________

Food for chickens to eat:

FABLE STRAPS ______________________

BORN ______________________

BOOKED WISH ______________________

GROSS and WEEPS ______________________

Chickens' personalities:

CALF ______________________

QUILT ______________________

THY ______________________

START ______________________

Ways to cook eggs:

LARD-BOWLED ______________________

COACHED ______________________

SCRAMBLER ______________________

SOFA-TOILED ______________________

Chicken terms:

EGO IN SOUR PACE ______________________ [embarrassed]

THICK SLICK ______________________ [movie that females like]

BATCH AT IDES ______________________ [be creative]

THICKEN FEUD ______________________ [small amount of money]

Code Jokes

Use the instructions to decode these jokes. Once you've solved them, try using the codes to send your friends secret messages.

1.

This first one is pretty simple – the joke's answer is spelled out by circling every letter that's immediately to the right of an "X." Then read the circled letters left to right, top to bottom.

Why did the chicken cross the floor of the apple juice factory?

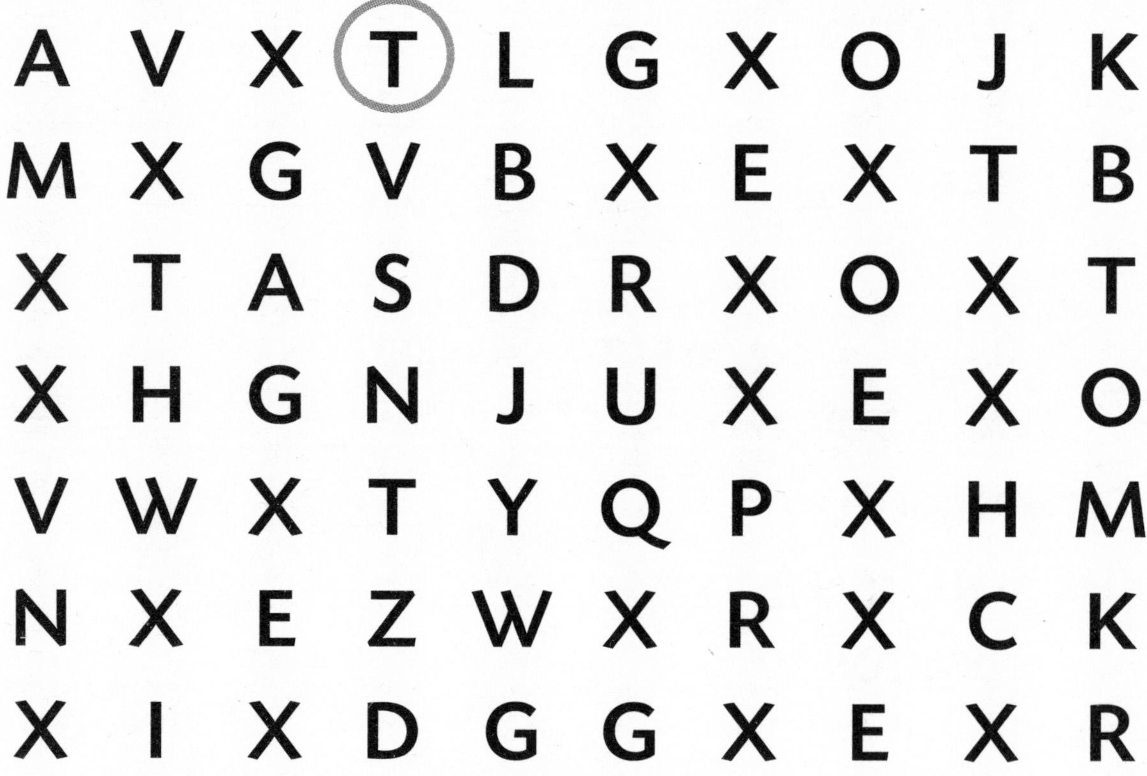

A	V	X	T	L	G	X	O	J	K
M	X	G	V	B	X	E	X	T	B
X	T	A	S	D	R	X	O	X	T
X	H	G	N	J	U	X	E	X	O
V	W	X	T	Y	Q	P	X	H	M
N	X	E	Z	W	X	R	X	C	K
X	I	X	D	G	G	X	E	X	R

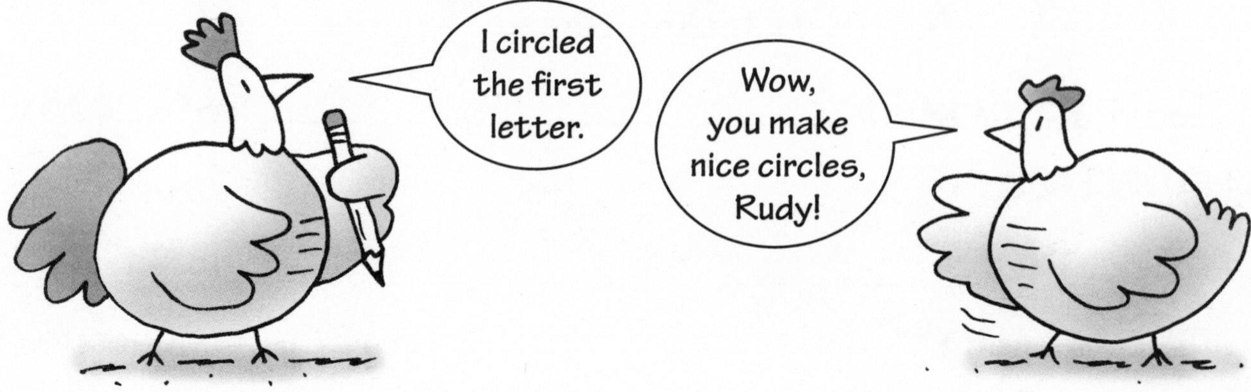

I circled the first letter.
Wow, you make nice circles, Rudy!

2.

Okay, let's take that idea and make it a little trickier. This time, circle each letter that's immediately to the right of ANY letter in the word CHICK. Then read the circled letters left to right, top to bottom.

What do you call factories where hens work?

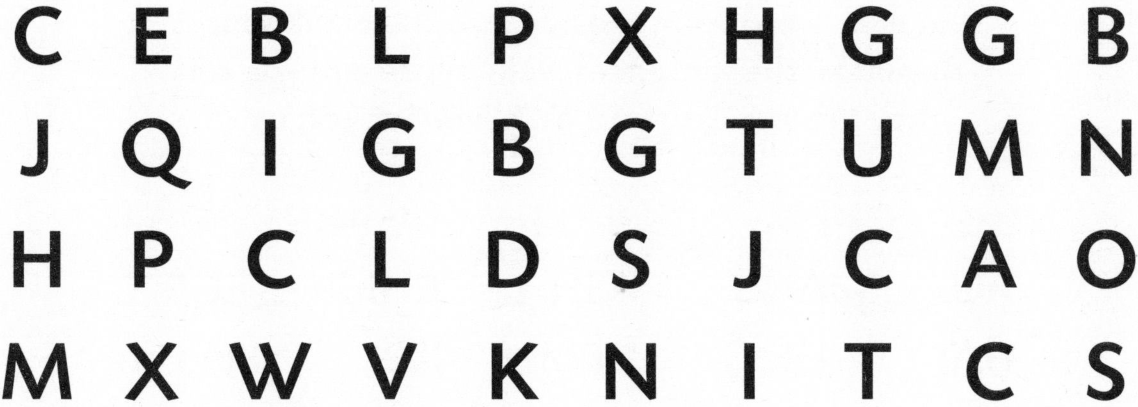

3.

Here's one last variation. Circle every letter that's immediately to the LEFT of two X's in a row (reading across). One X doesn't count, it has to be two in a row! Then read the circled letters from RIGHT to LEFT, top to bottom.

What do you call crazy chickens?

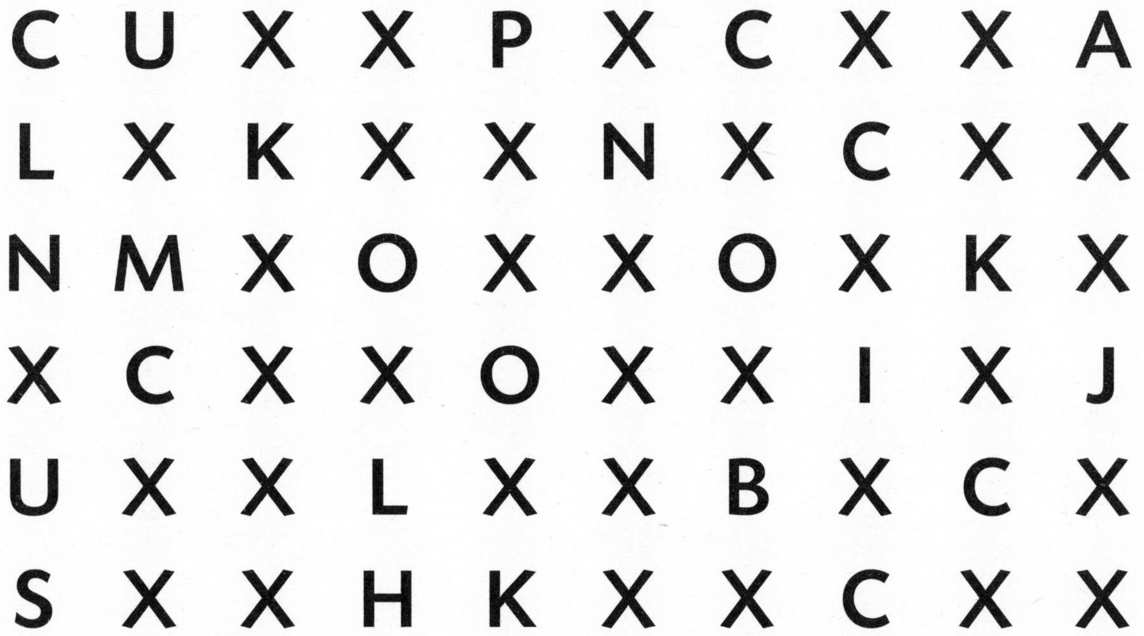

Rules, Rules

So, you want to raise chickens in an urban area? Before you get started it's a good idea to know the local laws for your community. Four of them are posted here, but some playful chicks removed 25 words from the list.

Put each word from the box into the blank spaces so that all the sentences make sense and you can obey the law. Cross off each word as you use it.

ALL	AND	ASH	CHICK	EGG
HAT	HE	HEM	ILL	IN
IT	LAW	MA	NEIGH	NOW
OFF	ON	OR	OUCH	OUR
OWN	SING	USE	WAY	YOU

1. K_ _ _ T_ _ ANI_ _L

Z_ _ING _ _ _ _S F_ _ Y_ _ _

C_ _Y OR T_ _ _.

2. DO NOT _ _ _OW CHICKENS

_ _SIDE YOUR HO_ _ _.

3. AL_ _ _S W_ _ _ YOUR

H_ _ _S AFTER T_ _ _ _ING

_ _ _ _ _ENS.

4. TELL _ _ _R _ _ _ _ _BORS

T_ _ _ YOU W_ _ _ BE

RAI_ _ _ _ CHICKENS AND

_ _ _ER TO GIVE T_ _ _

FRESH _ _ _S.

Sixers

Combine two 3-LETTER PIECES, one after the other, to form an answer for each clue. Write the answer in the grid reading ACROSS. The first has been done for you.

Reading DOWN, the letters in the gray squares will spell out a grooming method used by chickens.

Oh, I see.
BOI + LED
makes the first
answer.

3-LETTER PIECES

ANA	BAN	BER	~~BOI~~
CAR	EAS	GAT	HER
KIE	~~LED~~	LLS	LUM
SHE	SIL	TER	TON

Clue						
Cooked in very hot water, like eggs	B	O	I	L	E	D
Material for a chicken coop						
A chicken breed that sounds like a soft fabric						
Spring holiday featuring egg hunts						
A fruit that can be fed to chickens						
Container for holding eggs						
Collect (eggs)						
Outside coverings of eggs						

Match and Mix

Each chicken term below can be spelled by combining TWO words from the box and then rearranging the letters. For example, MAN and BAT could be combined to spell BANTAM.

ACTION	AND	BAGEL	CHIN
CLING	CROCK	DIG	EEL
FEAR	GREEN	NUTS	LAW
ROSE	ROT	RUB	TEST

1. BLEACHING = ______________ + ______________
2. WATTLES = ______________ + ______________
3. COCKEREL = ______________ + ______________
4. INCUBATOR = ______________ + ______________
5. ROOSTER = ______________ + ______________
6. CANDLING = ______________ + ______________
7. DUSTING = ______________ + ______________
8. FREE-RANGE = ______________ + ______________

To test whether you know what these terms mean, turn the page to check out our Dictionary Quiz.

The dictionary is filled with words and phrases that were used in the puzzles you've just done.
Cover up the definitions on the right and see how many words you know. Close enough counts!

Dictionary Quiz

A Dictionary and Word Quiz in One!

Do it for fun—or keep score.

To score, put a check mark in the box next to every word you get correct, then see how you rate on page 120.

We're easy graders—even five correct answers is good!

☐	**ALEKTOROPHOBIA**	Fear of chickens
☐	**BEAK**	Pointy chicken part used for eating and pecking
☐	**BLEACHING**	Fading of some parts on a chicken, such as the beak
☐	**CANDLING**	Looking inside an egg's shell using a strong light source, such as a candle
☐	**CAPE**	The narrow feathers between a chicken's back and head
☐	**CHICKEN WIRE**	Type of metal-wire fencing material used for pens
☐	**COCKEREL**	Male chicken under one year of age
☐	**COMB**	Fleshy crown on top of a chicken's head, usually red
☐	**COOP**	House for chickens

☐	**CRICKET**	Chirping, leaping insect
☐	**DUSTING/ DUSTBATH**	Wiggling around in the dirt to clean the feathers and get rid of bugs and tiny pests
☐	**FLUFF**	The fluffy part of a chicken above its legs
☐	**FLY THE COOP**	To run off or escape
☐	**FREE-RANGE**	Allowed to roam freely, outside a caged area
☐	**GIZZARD**	Part of a chicken's stomach used for grinding up food
☐	**HARD-BOILED**	Cooked, as an egg in a shell, so that it's firm inside
☐	**HEN HOUSE**	Chicken coop for hens to lay their eggs
☐	**HOBBY FARMER**	One who farms (or raises chickens) for fun

	Term	Definition
☐	**HOCK**	Joint on a chicken's leg similar to a human's ankle
☐	**HOEDOWN**	A square dance
☐	**INCUBATOR**	Device used to warm and hatch eggs
☐	**JERSEY GIANT**	Breed of chicken
☐	**KALE**	Dark green vegetable similar to lettuce
☐	**MEALWORM**	Young form of beetle sometimes fed to chickens
☐	**NEST EGG**	Fake egg put in a nest to encourage laying; also money saved for later
☐	**PLYMOUTH ROCK**	Chicken breed or where the Pilgrims landed in the U.S.
☐	**RULE THE ROOST**	To be in control, especially at home

☐	**SADDLE**	Part of a chicken's back just in front of the tail
☐	**SHANK**	Part of a chicken's leg between the claw and first joint
☐	**SICKLES**	Long, curved tail feathers on a rooster
☐	**SPECKLED**	Covered with lots of little spots of color
☐	**SPUR**	Sharp, pointy part on the back of a chicken's leg
☐	**WALK ON EGGSHELLS**	Be very careful, trying not to upset anyone
☐	**WATTLES**	Fleshy flaps that hang below a chicken's beak
☐	**WING**	Chicken "arm" used for flying

HOW DID YOU DO?

Count up your check marks and turn the page to find out.

Dictionary Quiz

The results:

There are 35 words in our dictionary. Count one point for every correct answer and see how you rate:

5	Good
10	Great
15	Terrific!
20	Wow!!!
25+	Are you a chicken?

The Answers

1

DAWN

1. Breakfast!

2. Checking In

Which side of a chicken has more feathers?

The outside

3. Off-Course

Riddle: What do you call a chicken at the North Pole?

Answer: Lost

4. Order! Order!

5. Wake-Up Call

An alarm cluck

6. Yum or Yuck!

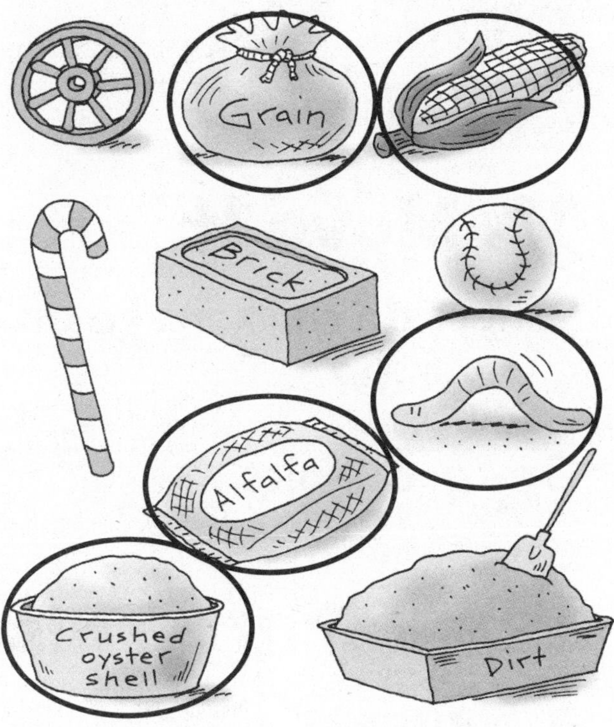

7. Chicken Feed

Mealworms

8. What's the Difference?

9. Find My Dad!

It's #4.

10. Mirror ɿoɿɿiM

Why did the chicken cross the playground?
To get to the other slide.

Why did the chicken cross the Internet?
To get to the other site.

Why did the horse cross the road?
The chicken needed a day off.

11. Move It

Where do chickens go on weekends?

On "peck"-nics.

12. Picture This

A. boots
B. glove
C. apron
D. window

Orpington

13. Barnyard Dash

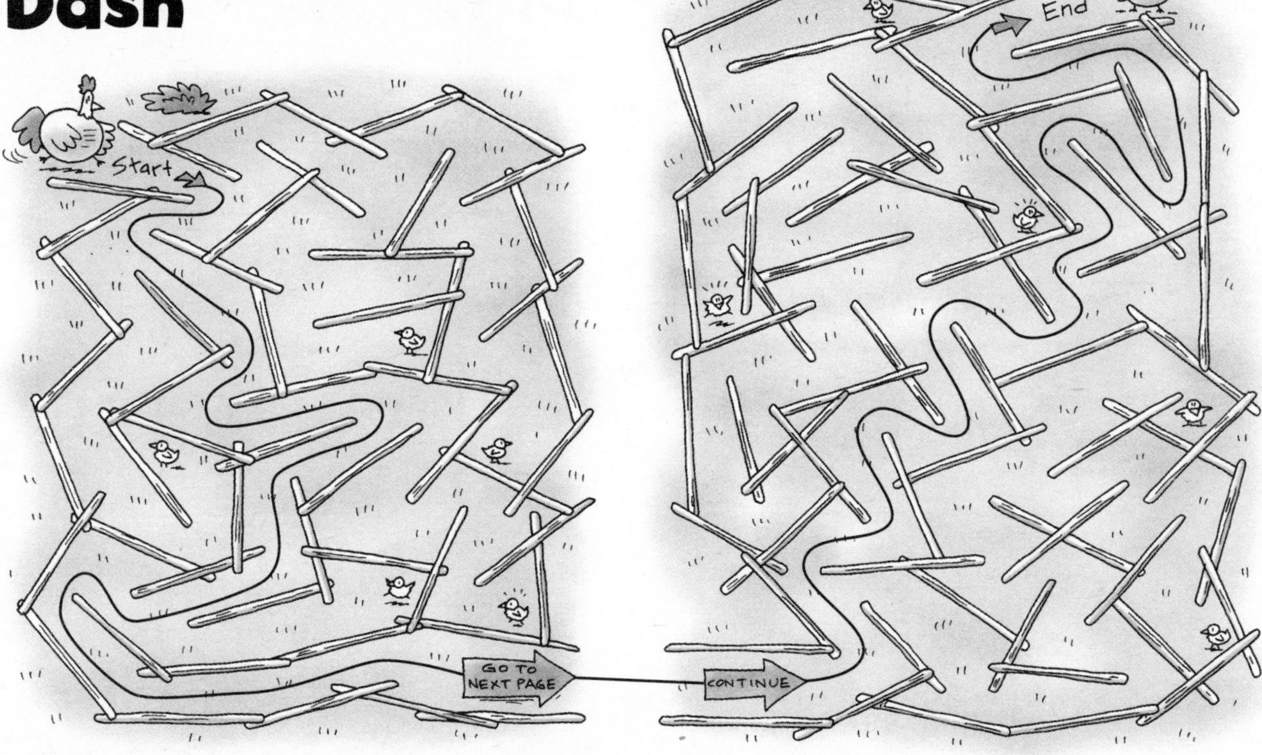

14. Beak Breakers

1. B chickens choose chow
2. G rooster rooter booster
3. E whose hands hold hens
4. A fumbling farmboy
5. F peach pit pie pitch
6. D cackle, cluck, crackle
7. C big black basket

15. Starting Line

a good egg

16. Choices

17. House Mates

Circled one matches.
Arrows show differences.

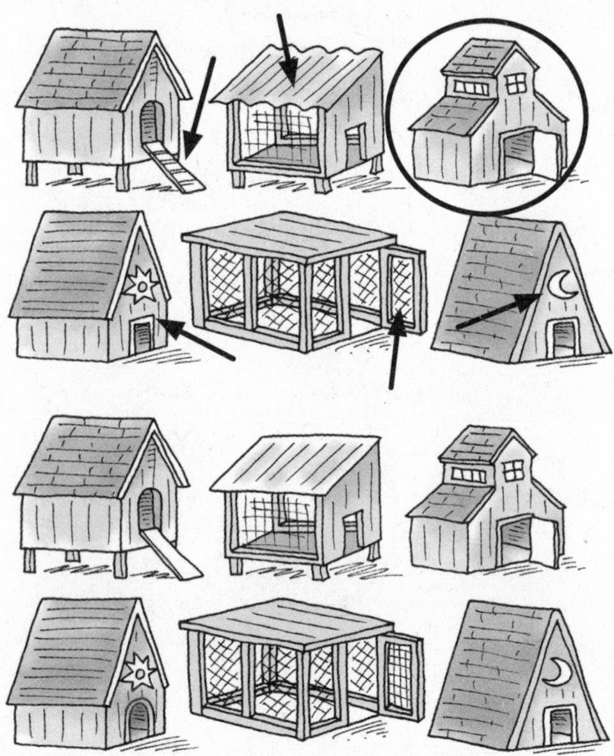

18. Name that Chick

19. Triple Treat

1. How did the egg cross the road?
It scrambled across.

2. What do you get if you cross a hen with a dog?
Pooched eggs.

3. Which fairy tales are the best? The ones with happy eggings.

20. Threesies

China

2 DAY

21. P-P-Puzzle

pine tree, plane, path, plant, pot, pig, paddle, pond, pineapple, picnic, (picnic table, picnic bench), plate, pepper, pizza, pie, pepperoni, and pillow (park also counts, and any others you might get)

22. The Mayflower Chicken

Plymouth Rock

23. Riddle Fun

May	road
big	ouch
pie	hand
hate	night
won	sick
nap	fudge
ace	goat
them	

Riddle: What do you get if a pig and a chicken bump into each other?

Answer: Ham and eggs.

24. Just Joking

Riddle 1: What Illinois city has lots of chickens?

Answer: Chick - cago.

Riddle 2: What do chickens serve at birthday parties?

Answer: Coop cakes.

25. Hen Scratching

1. C 2. E 3. B
4. D 5. A

26. Around and Around

It laid a sidewalk.

27. Finishing Line

a spring chicken

28. Reading Material

hencylopedia

29. Same Letters

1. F and I
2. C and G
3. B and J
4. A and L
5. D and K
6. E and H

30. Photo Match

Number 4 matches the original.

31. A Cheese-y Puzzle

32. Picture Pieces

A4 E4 A1 C1

D2 D4 A3 E5

F3 D1 C5 B1

B3 B5 A2 A5

33. Doubles

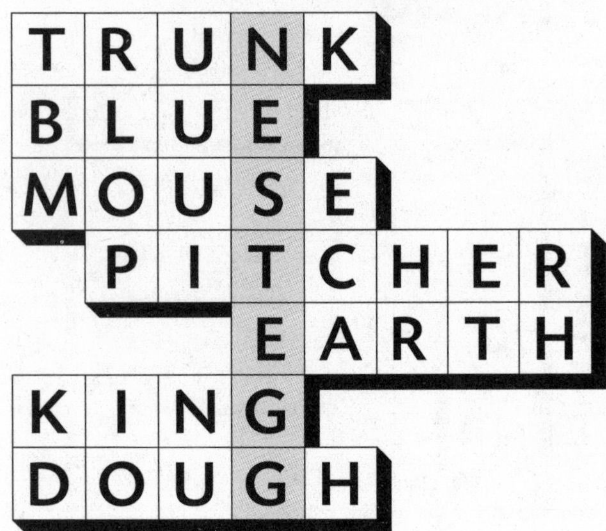

34. Remember

1. one pound
2. two 3. yes
4. corn, barley, or flowers
5. cow 6. white 7. two

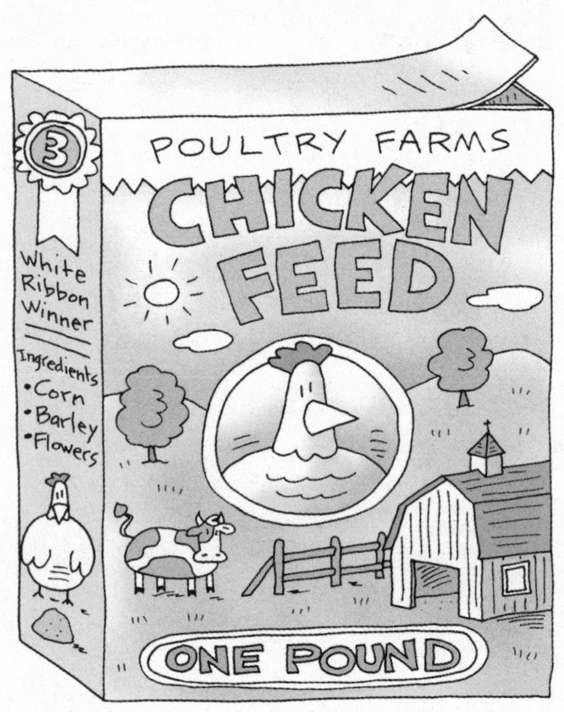

35. In Plain Sight

1. strap
2. dog
3. sat
4. hen
5. ring
6. hand
7. fall
8. car
9. cane
10. ram
11. wade
12. yam
13. pen
14. mug

36. Food for Thought

gizzard

37. State Bird

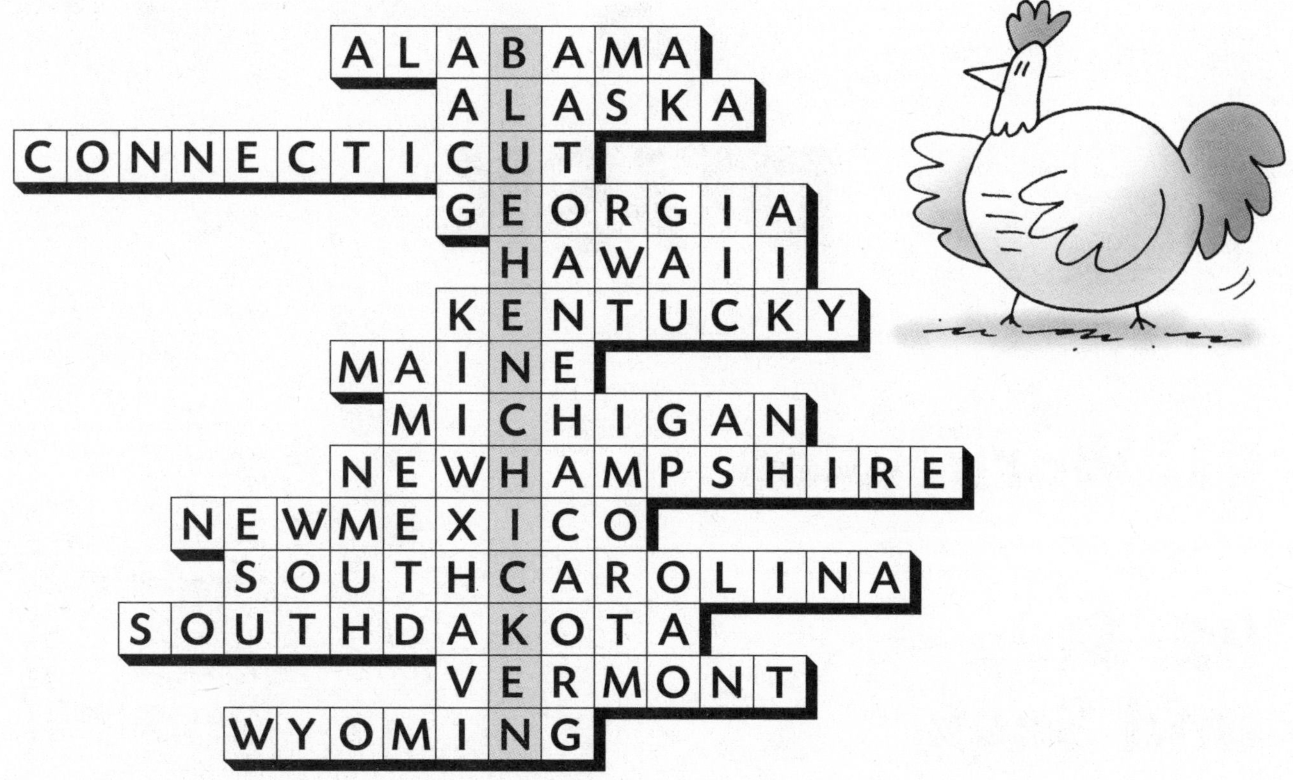

38. What a Treat!

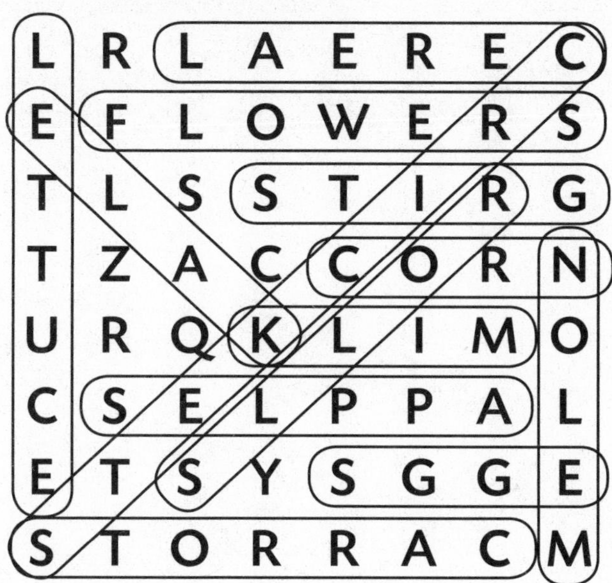

39. Cluckers

1. C 2. A 3. E
4. D 5. B

40. Step by Step

Riddle: What is always broken before it is used?

Answer: An egg.

3
DUSK

41. Wormholes

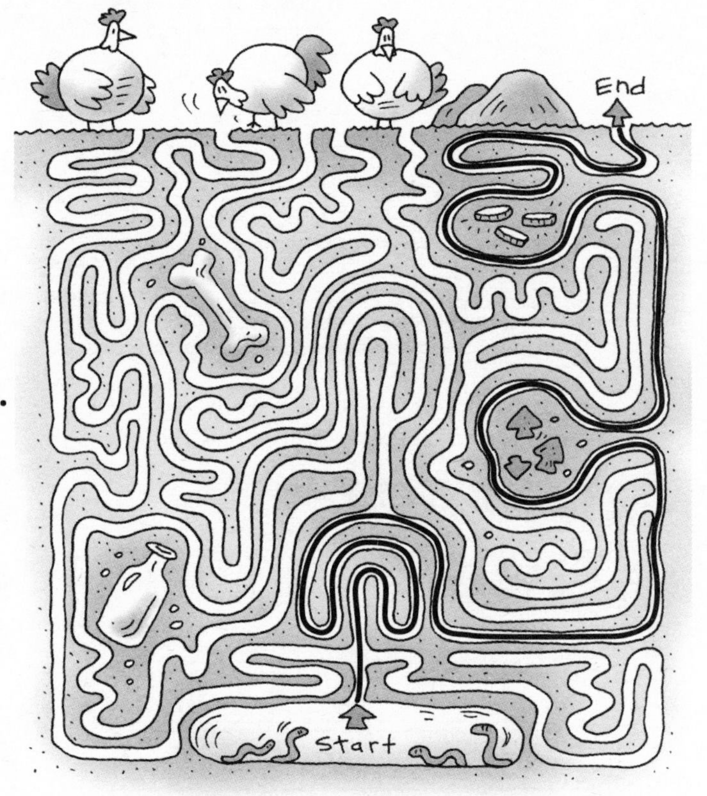

42. Hide and Seek

They wanted to ch<u>ase el</u>ephants.

The <u>corn is h</u>igh in the field.

Which <u>minor ca</u>n play ball?

They read the la<u>st ar</u>ticle.

Is <u>Nan kin</u>d? Yes.

She bought a <u>red cap</u>e.

They went to <u>camp in E</u>ngland.

O<u>mar ans</u>wered all the questions.

Take a ca<u>b and a ra</u>ilroad to get there.

Is the advi<u>ser a ma</u>th teacher?

Tho<u>se bright</u> kids got great marks.

In Guate<u>mala y</u>oung people play soccer.

43. Part Time

44. Following Directions

1. CATALANA
2. CTLN
3. COTLON
4. COSLON
5. COSELON
6. ROSELON
7. ROSELOM
8. ROSECOM
9. ROSECOMB

45. Talking Turkey

46. Name that Place

musical
vanish
turnpike
palace
elevator
half
earth
southwest
strong
Florida
leopard

Answer: Chickentown

47. Free-Range Fun

48. More Riddle Fun

city
bag
duck
write
Dutch
swims
teacher
show
cents
house
cake
done
thigh

Riddle: Why did the chewing gum cross the road?

Answer: Because it was stuck to the chicken.

49. Scaredy Cat

alektorophobia

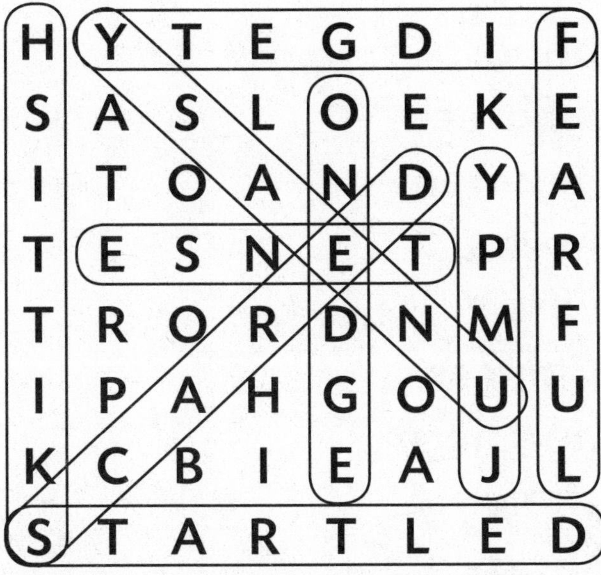

50. Imagine It

After you've memorized a list, don't look at it for a day and then see how you do. You might surprise yourself.

Make a list and trade it for a friend's list. See how you do memorizing each other's list.

51. Farm Walk

Buttercup's path:

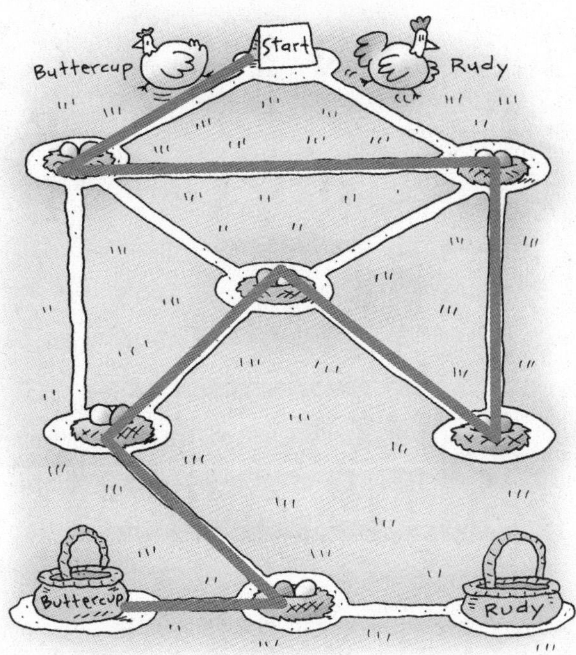

Rudy's path:

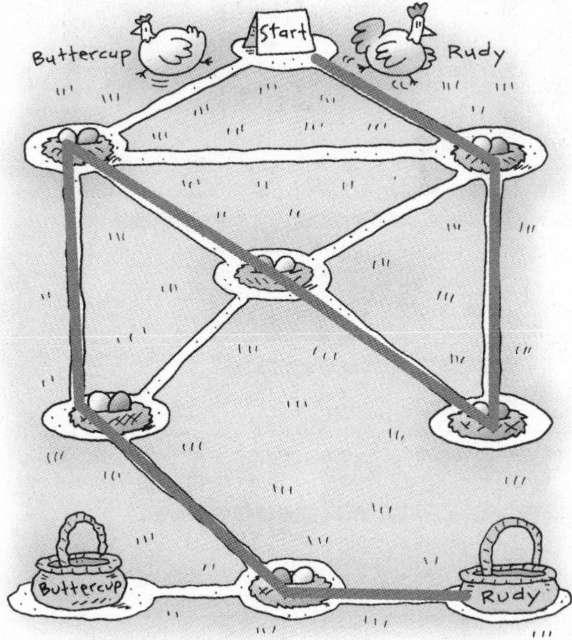

52. Double Trouble

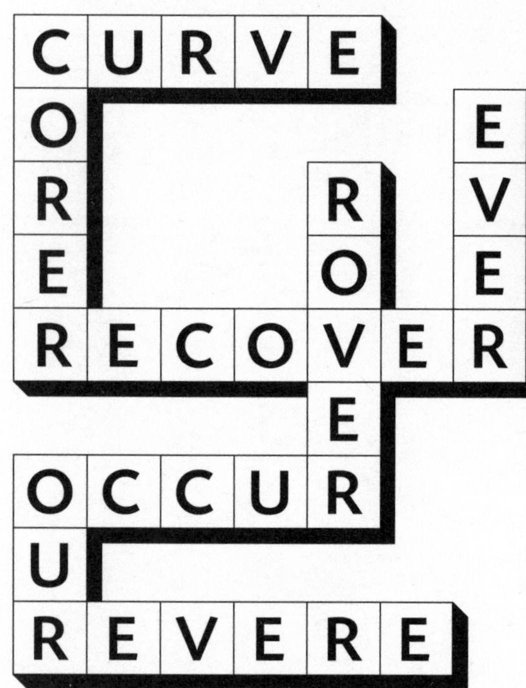

53. The Hen Zone

inches
honey
honest
eighteen
haunted
hyena
when
Chinese
northern
shine
shorten
frighten

54. Express Yourself

fly the coop
rule the roost

55. Who Am I?

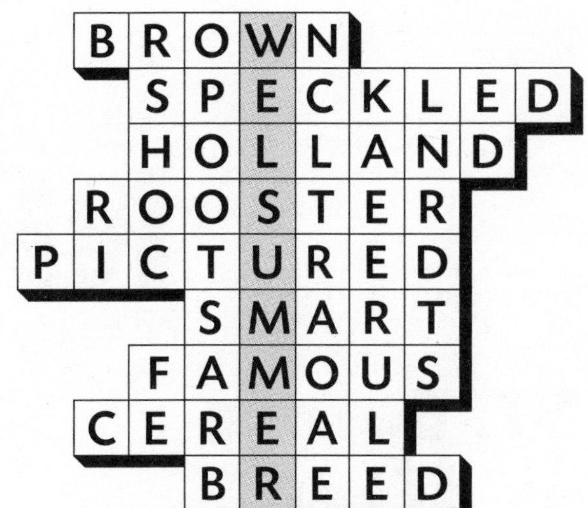

56. Funky Chicken

Numbers 2 and 7 are exactly the same.

next page →

4

NIGHT

57. Before or After

Riddle: Why don't chickens play baseball?

Answer: Because they always hit fowl balls.

58. Chicken Wire

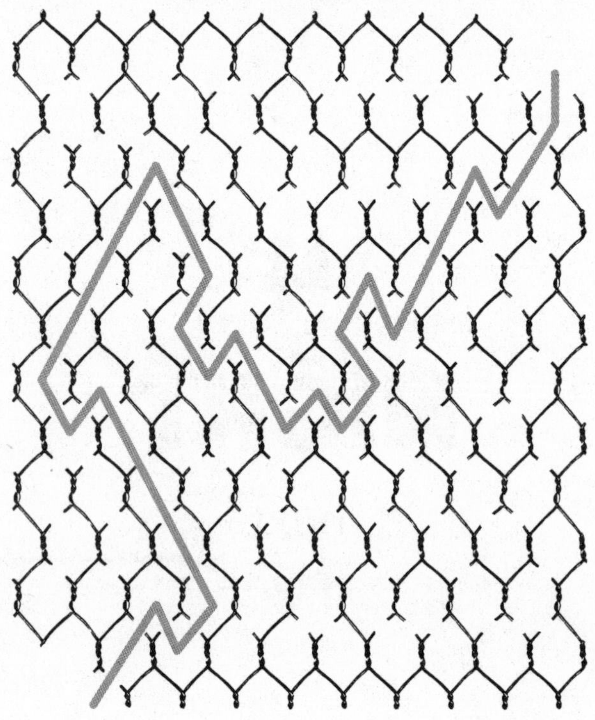

59. Chicken Sudoku

1.

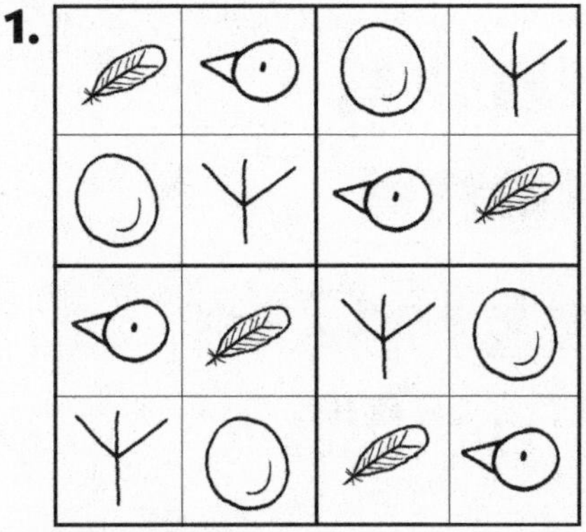

2.

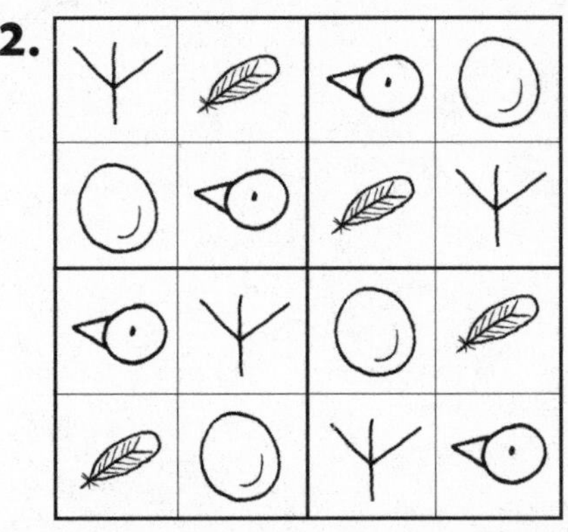

3.

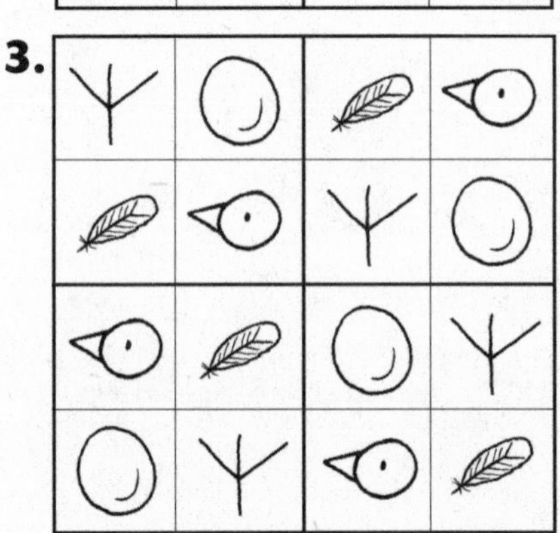

60. Spare Time

keychains
coins
bottle caps
buttons
toys
stuffed animals
model cars
marbles
stamps
stickers
autographs
baseball cards

hobby farmers

61. Globe Trotting

an eggs-plorer

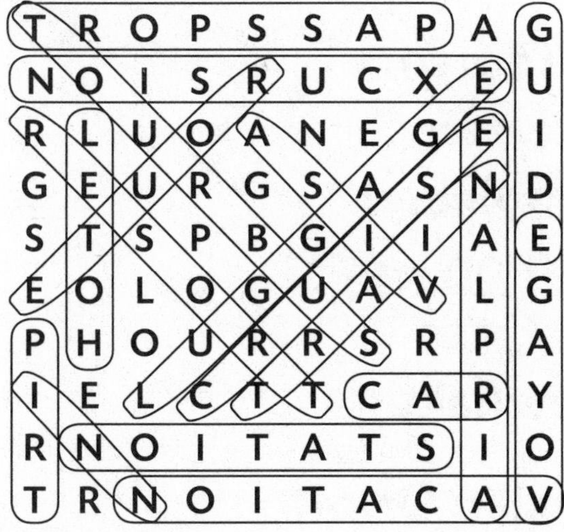

62. Get Rid of It

1. cluck
2. instant
3. polite
4. grumpy
5. sweat
6. neighbor
7. silent
8. exercise
9. ant
10. stroll
11. thin
12. seldom
13. chapter
14. fragile

Leftovers:
No bet so she ether wide.

Answer:
To get to the other tide.

63. True/False

Matilda

64. Chicken Coupe

A. 4
B. 3
C. 1
D. 7
E. 6
F. 2
G. 8
H. 5

Here's what was removed in number 2, 3, and so on:

65. Sicilian Buttercup

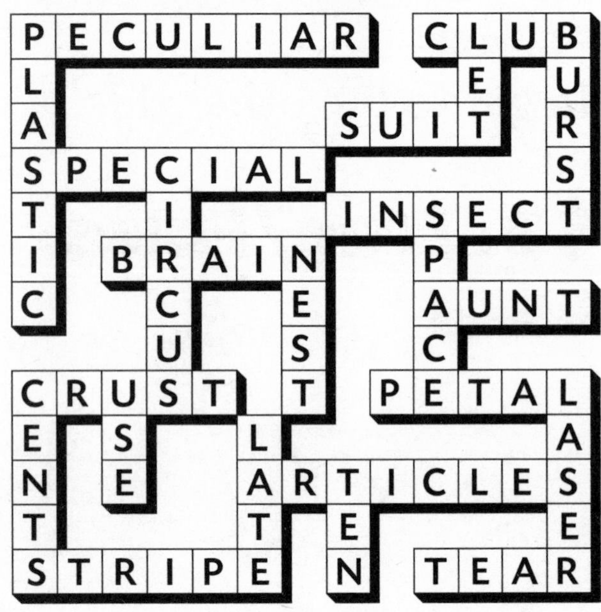

66. Egg Match

67. Rare Breed

geography
hamburger
classical
admission
continent
quotation
adventure

custodian
entertain
bumblebee
harmonica
briefcase
snowflake

Russian Orloff

68. Missing in Action

Barnevelder
Buckeye
Rhode Island Red
Catalana
Rosecomb
Andalusian
Dorking
Campine
Hamburg
Leghorn
Sumatra
Welsummer

Chantecler
Phoenix
Sebright
Redcap
Orpington
Plymouth Rock
Jersey Giant
Faverolle
Lakenvelder
New Hampshire Red
Delaware
Cornish

69. Close Relatives

nails, lumber, chicken wire, roofing

hammer, power drill, saw, ruler

blue-green, creamy white, dark brown, speckled

table scraps, corn,
cooked fish,
grass and weeds

calm, quiet, shy, smart

hard-boiled, poached, scrambled, soft-boiled

egg on your face,
chick flick, hatch an idea,
chicken feed

70. Code Jokes

1. to get to the other cider
2. eggplants
3. cuckoo clucks

71. Rules, Rules

1. Know the animal zoning laws for your city or town.

2. Do not allow chickens inside your house.

3. Always wash your hands after touching chickens.

4. Tell your neighbors that you will be raising chickens and offer to give them fresh eggs.

72. Sixers

dustbath

B	O	I	L	E	D
L	U	M	B	E	R
S	I	L	K	I	E
E	A	S	T	E	R
B	A	N	A	N	A
C	A	R	T	O	N
G	A	T	H	E	R
S	H	E	L	L	S

73. Match and Mix

1. bleaching = bagel + chin
2. wattles = law + test
3. cockerel = crock + eel
4. incubator = action = rub
5. rooster = rose + rot
6. candling = and + cling
7. dusting = dig + nuts
8. free-range = green + fear

Alphabetical List of Contents

page number • puzzle title • (puzzle number)

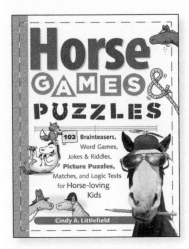

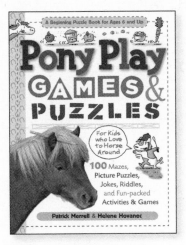

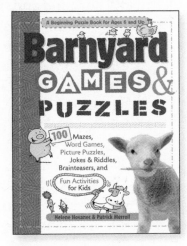

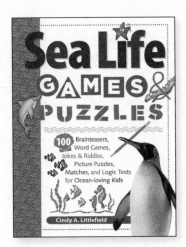

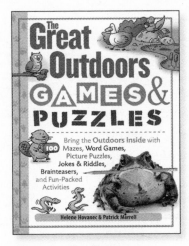